Gravity Hill

GRAVITY HILL
MAXIMILIAN WERNER

A MEMOIR

THE UNIVERSITY OF UTAH PRESS
Salt Lake City

The Defiance House Man colophon is a registered trademark of the University of Utah Press. It is based on a four-foot-tall Ancient Puebloan pictograph (late PIII) near Glen Canyon, Utah.

17 16 15 14 13   1 2 3 4 5

Library of Congress Cataloging-in-Publication Data

Werner, Maximilian.
 Gravity Hill / Maximilian Werner.
   pages cm
 ISBN 978-1-60781-242-5 (paper : alkaline paper)
 ISBN 978-1-60781-243-2 (ebook)
 1. Werner, Maximilian—Childhood and youth. 2. Werner, Maximilian—Mental health. 3. Salt Lake City (Utah)—Biography. 4. Teenagers—Utah—Salt Lake City—Biography. 5. Subculture—Utah—Salt Lake City—History—20th century. 6. Marginality, Social—Salt Lake City—History—20th century. 7. Mormons—Utah—Salt Lake City—History—20th century. 8. Suburban life—Utah—Salt Lake City—History—20th century. 9. Salt Lake City (Utah)—Social conditions—20th century. 10. Salt Lake City (Utah)—Social life and customs—20th century. I. Title.
 F834.S253W47 2013
 979.2>258033—dc23

                                                                2012037040

Cover painting: *Natural History,* by Bradford Overton © 2012. Used by permission of the artist. Art direction for cover painting by Audrey Z. Smith. Cover design by Jessica A. Booth.

Printed and bound by Sheridan Books, Inc., Ann Arbor, Michigan

IN MEMORY OF TRAVIS MERRILL

HERETOFORE I HAVE BEEN TRYING TO SAVE MY PRECIOUS HIDE,
TRYING TO PRESERVE THE FEW PIECES OF MEAT THAT HID MY BONES.
I AM DONE WITH THAT. I HAVE REACHED THE LIMITS OF ENDURANCE.
MY BACK IS TO THE WALL; I CAN RETREAT NO FURTHER.

—HENRY MILLER, TROPIC OF CANCER

CONTENTS

ACKNOWLEDGMENTS

I thank John Alcock and Daniel Wallace for graciously reading and responding to this and every book I have ever written, and for offering their insightful and pointed feedback. I thank them also for their friendship.

My editor John Alley deserves my gratitude for his suggestions and for believing in me and in *Gravity Hill*. Thanks also to Glenda Cotter and the good people at the University of Utah Press for their role in helping me realize this book.

A warm thanks to James Anker of Barclay Creek Press, and especially to Mark Bailey and Kirsten Allen of Torrey House Press. They've been with me on this journey and it has been a privilege to know and work with them.

AUTHOR'S NOTE

This is a work of creative nonfiction. I have tried to write a book that is aesthetically pleasing and true. The extent to which I have succeeded in the first case shall of course be decided by the reader, but the book is in fact true. I have freely revealed myself without censure, but in order to protect the privacy of the other people who wander these pages, I have changed their names and some of the surrounding details of their lives. The reader is invited to ponder the contents of this book and their implications, but my hope is that at no time will the reader ever doubt the truthfulness of these events.

PART ONE

TRILLIUM

I'D LIKE IT HERE IF I COULD LEAVE
AND SEE YOU FROM A LONG WAY AWAY.
—MICHAEL STIPE

The sound of parenthood is the sigh. Late last night, my eleven-month-old daughter, Greer, awoke disquieted. Whether because of foul dreams or hunger, it is not unusual for her to awaken several times a night. Unconcerned, I listened while Kim tried to console and nurse her back to sleep. "It's okay," Kim whispered sweetly, as she tried without success to interest Greer in nursing. Within moments, Greer's crying intensified, until finally Kim got up and carried her out of the room, not so much for my sake—I was wide awake and she knew it—but for the sake of our three-year-old son, Wilder, who, after four joyous months of sleeping in his own bed, has returned to our bed with a renewed vigor, represented by the pillow and sippy-cup of water he brings with him each night when he's finished playing in his room. When I asked Wilder to explain the sudden change, he claimed his bed is too small. But given the sliver he now occupies in our bed (except, of course, when he sleeps horizontally, with his head on Kim's pillow and his feet on mine), I suspect there must be more to it. For now he was fast asleep, and so I laid there as Kim and Greer moved from room to room like a fire spreading throughout the house. Spending as much time together as they do, the two are very close, and Kim is expert in deciphering Greer's plaintive grunts and whines. Usually Kim tries to calm Greer with soothing words and something in the environment, such as a toy, magazine, or toothbrush. When that doesn't work, out comes the breast. Once or twice Greer has, like her brother before her, expectantly sampled my nipples and found them poor, hairy substitutes. Nevertheless, Kim has been the only provider of nutrient-rich comfort. But there have been times when Greer's distress cannot be assuaged by breast-feeding. Lying in the darkness, listening to things go from bad to worse, I became more and more anxious, until finally I was no longer willing to eavesdrop.

I got up, put on my robe, and tucked my pillow next to Wilder so that he wouldn't roll off the bed. Now that I am a father, how many times will I feel like I want to die? I don't mean permanently. I mean finding a way to justify living despite the stupid things I do. The first time I wanted to be dead in this temporary way was when Wilder and I were home alone and he wriggled off the bed. I'm not exactly sure how old he was at the time, perhaps four or five months, but he was still young enough that he wasn't moving much and neither Kim nor I thought twice about napping him on the bed. Kim was at work. I was in the living room talking on the phone with my mother. I heard a small thud and, horrified by what I knew it meant, I ran in the bedroom.

Wilder was lying face-down on the floor in the fetal position, crying softly. At the time, I believed that infants could be too easily broken, so I picked him up carefully and examined his head and body. I was afraid he had hit the nightstand on the way down, but I couldn't find any evidence of impact. Based on how I found him, I hoped his folded arms and legs had cushioned his fall. Ultimately he seemed fine, like he was still half asleep and just wanted to finish his nap. But something in me wouldn't let me see that he was alright. My body was in upheaval. I held him and walked throughout the house in a state of guilt-inspired madness. I remember telling Wilder over and over how sorry I was as I pressed him to my chest and stroked his little head. I finally managed to pick up the phone and call Kim, who promptly left work and drove home. She would later confess that she was more concerned about me than about Wilder. I know she meant well, but I knew I had failed to protect the most important thing in the world.

I got knocked down. But here I was again, over three years later, getting up to do what I could for my stricken, eleven-month-old daughter. I found Kim and Greer in the kitchen and instantly I was struck by Greer's anguished appearance: her normally placid, doll-like face was purple-red and her eyes were swollen and shut tight against the world. If all I had to go on were this moment, I would not recognize my own daughter. Instinctively, I reached for her, and as I clasped my hands around her warm little torso, I asked Kim what she thought was wrong. I didn't hear her, though, because then I saw that her own face was a somber pond of worry and fatigue, which was underscored by the inflamed rims of her eyelids. Inasmuch as Kim is the barometer within the familial ecosystem, things were looking bleak. Panic built in my chest, as if a cord was wrapping round and round my heart. Before panic could spread to the rest of my body, I turned to Greer and called her name. Perhaps responding to the alarm and mild anger in my voice, she became more agitated and cried even harder.

I quickly tried to undo the damage by rubbing her head and whispering to her. As I moved her hair away from her eyes, I felt the damp crying-heat of her forehead. "It's like she's still asleep," Kim said, standing off to the side with her arms loosely folded. The shadows crossed her face and her skin was so pale that for an instant I wondered if she were really there. I then imagined I was a single father and that Kim's ghost stayed on to help me. I noted the dryness in my mouth and my heart knocking around in my throat. I felt like I had to get away, to escape to another life where I was not a father, where I was not this version of myself. I withdrew and waited for an alternative to emerge. Would I have a beard in this new life of mine? Call rivers, wolves, and ravens my neighbors? Would the dirt be my floor? The sky my roof?

"Does she feel hot to you?" Kim asked, returning me to the crisis of the moment.

I pressed my cheek to Greer's forehead. "Not really." It occurred to me that there might be a spider in her diaper or beneath her jammies. "Did you check her diaper?"

Kim looked confused, not because of the question, but because of the accusatory way I asked it.

"Yes, I did."

I took Greer down the hall and into the bathroom, where we tried running her a bath.

By then Kim and I were both at the height of our stress, and the sound of the water crashing into the tub and into the jumbled heap of bright toys and magnetic letters made everything seem worse. A pubic hair coiled like an invasive, serpent stowaway on the bow of a toy boat. Kim often teases that the hairs we find are always mine, and that we could weave a small rug with them, charges I flatly deny. It is one of the last running jokes we still share.

When we used to go fly-fishing, I would wait until we were fifty miles out of town to ask Kim if she remembered to pack the fishing rods. Packing the truck was not her responsibility, and that is what made the joke funny. I haven't had an opportunity to try that joke for four years, not since Kim was about six months pregnant with Wilder. Those days of fishing together were some of our finest. As much as I love replaying them in my mind, I think we've both gotten used to them being gone.

Over the noise of the water and Greer's crying, Kim and I debated whether to leave on the bathroom light.

"It's too much," I said, lightly bouncing Greer and holding her away from the light.

"It might help her to—" Kim started to say.

But I was out the door and on my way to the living room before Kim could finish her sentence. Alarmed by all the commotion, our youngest cat, Bella Jean, trotted down the dark hall. She was surprisingly noisy, a fact that I attributed to her troubling winter weight gain and to the thinness of our wood floors. If we hadn't gotten her spayed, I'd swear she was pregnant. Greer is fascinated by the cats, so I tried to alert her to Bella: "Look at the fat kitty." But she only seemed to get more upset. I felt like the wings of dark birds were fluttering in my throat and I knew my patience was slipping. As I passed our room, I looked in on Wilder. There was just enough moon and street light coming through the blinds to light his sleeping face.

I proceeded into the living room, as if by doing so I might escape and break the hold of all these troubling feelings. Greer and I would often stand in front of the stereo and listen to everything from Chopin to Pearl Jam. I would dance with her in my arms and she would hum along. Hearing the music, Wilder would quit whatever he was doing and eagerly join the rumpus, dancing around us, trying to snap his fingers and do cartwheels. But Greer and I were now standing in the dark and I knew she wanted nothing to do with music. It was as if she was trapped inside her own head and her eyes were the escape hatch she could not open.

And yet, as if according to some interior map, perhaps the one of the universe printed on the insides of her eyelids, she directed me here and there with an outstretched arm. Kim's body is shaped like an hourglass and the kids sit securely on her hip, but I must rely on my arms, which quickly tire when Greer leans and I've got to strain to keep her from falling. It was mentally exhausting as well because I knew that no matter where I took her, she would not be satisfied. "Where do you want to go, sweetheart?" I tried to put her down, get her walking, but then a hell of sound broke loose. I felt hot, anxious, and torn by my concern for Greer and by how desperately I wanted her to stop crying. There is no worse sound and I started to come apart.

The local news often reports on the father (seldom the mother) who either attempts to kill or succeeds in killing his crying child. But I know what is in my bones. When it comes to the well-being of my children, I want to believe my gentleness and fatherly love will always override my desperation. Luckily, Kim joined us and asked if she should take Greer to the emergency room. I could not avoid the anxiety in Kim's voice, but I was thankful for the darkness because it hid her face.

When Kim and I encounter moderate distress in either of our children, our tendency is to wait and see what happens. We each act as a check-and-balance, in an effort both to reassure one another (as well as the children) and to avoid unnecessary trips to the emergency room, which represent their own form of trauma. After a certain point, however, I have been known to resort to a kind of shotgun approach to resolving problems that are clearly beyond my control. Lacking the precise tool to deal with the issue at hand, I throw everything I have and hope something works. On more than one occasion, Kim has had to tell me to relax. If that doesn't work, she will demand that I leave the room. And that is exactly what I do. Who can stand the feeling of being so useless? This time, however, neither of us knew what to make of Greer's distress. Although dire, the situation did not seem to be getting worse, so in a moment of calm I suggested she call the doctor first and see what she said. "Okay," Kim said, and then disappeared into the office.

Greer's crying leveled off, but it still inspired dread. I could hear Kim in the office, answering the doctor's questions. "No, no fever," she said. "About two hours ago." I listened for a few more seconds, and when I didn't detect any changes in Kim's voice I searched the mantelpiece for a small box of wooden matches. "There they are," I whispered to Greer. I shook the box and, though she continued to cry, she opened her eyes long enough to reach for and then push away the matches.

Normally Greer would eagerly take the matches and pass them from hand to hand and study them with the curious eyes of a primate. Still, I knew this was a chance to break through to her, so before she closed her eyes, I took out a match and struck it. We were standing in front of the fireplace and a large mirror rested on the mantelpiece. Greer wouldn't look at me, but I saw her reflection wince as she whiffed the sulfur. For a moment she stopped crying, opened her green-brown eyes, and pointed to the match. "Kchee," she said. Instantly my breathing slowed and my jaw relaxed. I told myself that if anything were seriously wrong, a match's fire would not change it.

I kissed her hot cheek and smelled her skin. My nose told me she was mine. Then I described the climbing flame, the column of colors. Soon the match burned out, sending a thread of smoke spiraling into the dark room. "Where did the flame go?" I asked, lifting up Greer's pajamas to reveal her cream-white tummy. "Is it under here? No." Greer looked annoyed and in no mood to play. I took the hint. "Here it is." I slid open the match box, took out another match, and struck it. I'd been monitoring Kim's conversation in the other room, listening not so much to the words, but to the urgency with which they were spoken. When she rejoined us in the living room, Greer and I were standing in front of the big picture window. I had lit a candle and Greer and I were watching it flicker.

"How is she doing?" Kim asked. When Greer heard Kim's voice, she turned and leaned toward the sound.

"She's doing better," I said, handing her to Kim.

"What did the doctor say?"

Kim sat on the couch and cradled Greer as she nursed and soon fell back to sleep. "She thinks it was a night terror."

I blew out the candle, placed it on the mantel, and then sat down next to Kim. "Night terror?" I whispered as I smoothed back Greer's damp shock of hair.

"Yes."

Greer stirred at the sound of our voices and so our conversation ended, but later I would learn that night terrors are nonspecific, disembodied fears. Because they cannot be named, they cannot be confronted or destroyed, and that is what makes them so terrifying.

I looked outside and scanned the neighborhood. I focused on the large bush beneath my neighbor's tree, perhaps because each time I see it in the dark I think it's someone standing out there, watching us.

I keep getting it wrong. But then I started to wonder what a watcher would see. What would he think is going on in here, in this house of terror and flame and night? Despite my questionings, the world out there seemed no less distant: my neighbor's windows were filled with the same dark as me and the trees and the sky. Beneath them were luminous blue lawns of snow. It was all so frightening and so beautiful; the world outside my dry mouth, my walls, and my sleeping daughter.

★ ★ ★

My children have always been here, or so it seems. Last night before bed, I recalled a trip we took to the southern Utah desert. I tried to remember the details of the place and what my kids were doing as I set up camp and I saw them as if I were watching a grainy, black-and-white film. Then I realized that, as of this trip, Wilder and Greer had not even been born. Even when I imagine my life before them, they still travel the horizons of my dreams.

Kim and I had both dreamed about meeting Wilder long before he was born. We could never really say what he looked like, but when we knew he was coming we planned for life with him in it. Kim devoured books on parenting, birth, and pregnancy. She bought diapers, clothes, books, and toys. She ate the best food and went for long walks before the sun got too high. I did whatever I was told and imagined teaching him to fly-fish. I saw myself kneeling in the grass along the river so I could look him in the eye as I explained how to choose flies, tie knots, and read water. And when his face clouded at my mention of deceit, of tricking the trout into thinking what I want them to think, I would tell him that fooling a trout is not the same as fooling himself or other people. Including dreams and imaginings, Wilder was years in the making. But Greer just appeared, like a feather that falls from an empty sky.

Kim and I wanted a second child once our lives got back to normal, but as of our first summer back in Salt Lake, we just weren't ready. After living in Arizona for the past twelve years, we were now confronted with returning to old territory and building new lives. I felt like a member of the hunting party that travels for weeks and returns without any meat. Added to our personal wreckage was the utter improbability of conceiving. We just assumed that because it took twenty-five hundred dollars' worth of mild intervention—hormone shots, creams, pills, eye of newt—and over two years to conceive Wilder that the same would be true for our second child. Of course we were wrong. The night (or was it day?) Kim and I conceived Greer, we hadn't made love in over six months. I call it "lovemaking" as a matter of propriety, and out of respect for Kim, which is odd because I am fairly sure she wouldn't describe it as lovemaking either.

I think both Kim and I wish things had been better between us when we made Greer. I look at Wilder and I see those clear blue eyes and that sweet smile and I am proud of how hard we worked to get him here. I packed my balls in ice and Kim quit drinking coffee and, after we'd made love, stood on her head! Making Wilder was the most complete, intense, painful, and beautiful expression of needing either of us had known.

Compared to the story of Wilder's conception, Greer's story is hard to tell. Wilder and I were outside working in the garden when Kim brought out the little white dipstick and showed it to me. I know it was late in the day because of the color of the grass and how the light fell slantwise through the elms. As Wilder used his yellow toy shovel to dig for worms in the moist earth, Kim and I stood apart and cried strange tears.

After that, we both switched to autopilot and got to work. For me that meant getting my head right and cutting back on my drinking. For Kim it meant the usual, extraordinary self-sacrifice. I have never known another person who has understood so well the responsibility of growing a child. We wanted Greer. We just weren't expecting her to come when she did. The story of what happened before Greer has everything and nothing to do with her. The simple fact is that Greer is beautiful even if we are not.

Greer was still months away when we got into town in early April of 2006. After a brief and tumultuous stay at my mother's house—my mother said I was not the person she remembered, and I said, *You're right, Mother, I became a man*—Kim, Wilder, and I bought our own place in the Mill Creek area of Salt Lake. Self-described "recovering Mormons" live to our west, and two older women, Arlene and Deanne, and their four dogs live to our east. A young couple, practicing Mormons, lives directly north of us across the street. We all live just east of the cemetery, so apart from these people, most of our neighbors are the dead. The dead make good neighbors. The only noise they make is when their bodies fart deep underground, which no one hears anyway.

Of course, the cemetery is not without noise. A summer day does not go by that I don't hear bagpipes or guns commemorating a new arrival to the Subterranean Community. I have always been a sucker for *Amazing Grace,* and that first summer I would lean on my shovel or pause in my work and listen as the bagpipe rose out of the neighborhood cacophony of dog barks, lawn mowers, traffic, and children's laughter. My sweat would fall and wash the dust from the grass and sometimes the breeze would shift and I would hear bits of eulogies that were meaningful only to the people hearing them.

When it is winter, I am inside and I don't see much of what goes on at the cemetery. I imagine winter is the worst season to die or to attend someone's funeral. Funeral shoes aren't suitable for ice and snow. The mourners gather over there like a bouquet of black roses. I can't smell in the still winter air, so I am unsure if the older women are wearing heavy perfume. It is likely their fingers are shrinking in the cold and they are risking their jewels falling into the snow.

Winter would be an acceptable time to die if the sun were shining and I could see a tree with robins in it because their songs are tinged with melancholy and their bodies hold the light, reminding me of spring and of when I was a kid and all that really mattered was the moment. I'd like to phase out in the throes of a childhood memory. I don't want glass and gasoline. I don't want an empty road with blowing snow and wreckage spread down it and men standing around me who don't know my name. I would like a sweet memory if I have any left. If given time, the mind will empty its contents as it prepares to let go of life. Decent of it.

Whenever my time comes, I'd be more comfortable if my children weren't looking at me and assumed that my life had been worth something. Although I am not sure how much good that would do. Last December my friend Teegy sent me an image of himself, his wife, and their three young daughters. They are lying on their backs in Kentucky bluegrass and laughing in what has got to be evening in Tempe. It is quite possibly the most beautiful image of its kind. Moved, I called Teegy to thank him and he told me he had been sleeping with another woman and that he was going to leave his wife. Who would have thought?

Despite the falseness of appearances, I would also put on a face for my kids. Years later and sensing the truth, they would want an explanation and would knock lightly on the door of the sunny room in which Kim was sitting with a cat on her lap and looking out a window. Kim wouldn't hear the knock, though, because she would be concentrating on the song of a sparrow as it tilted back its head and gushed.

★ ★ ★

When my grandfather died, the birds were asleep and my mother glided through the dark house and woke me and my siblings. She gathered us into her room where we sat bewildered on her bed while she talked on the phone and cried. I think she was talking to one of her sisters, from whom she gathered the useless details of her father's death. "Was he awake? What did he say?" and "What time did he die? He's been dead all this time?" If I could get back to that night, I would take the phone from my mother's hand and return it to the receiver. Not fully awake or recognizing the significance of our mother's loss, my brother, sister, and I sat around her and whimpered. We brushed each other's hair and sang *Jesus loves me, this I know, for the Bible tells me so.*

We didn't really do that. But if we were someone else—perhaps my neighbors to the north and west and east—we might have and it might have given us some comfort. But there was no comfort to be had. And who is to say anything not the truth is a lie? At one time my mother might have knelt and prayed, but she stood and every so often I would catch glimpses of her face. I thought of astronauts cut loose in space. How odd it was, all of us sitting there together. I can't think of another time when we did that. Just sat together. I wonder how many years I would lose if I counted all the things I will never do again.

I didn't know my grandfather very well. I have a few memories of him. One of them is of him sitting on the toilet reading a newspaper. He's wearing his Mormon garments with the flap in the back. Apparently he left open the bathroom door to keep an eye on things. A week before he died, I stopped by his hospital room to say hello and goodbye. I was sixteen and on my way to a high school dance at the Utah state capitol. I was wearing some nice slacks, a white button-up shirt, a shitty tie, and my dead Uncle Steve's sports jacket. My mother tells me I looked like Steve when I was born. I think maybe she thought I *was* Steve, but only for a couple of seconds.

Steve was twenty-three when he died in a drunk-driving accident. Luckily, he had a son before he was killed by a speeding sugar beet truck. Unluckily, his son died under precisely the same circumstances. Same age. Drunk driving. Everything. If my grandfather recognized Steve's sports jacket, he didn't say so. He did, however, scold me for not cinching my tie before coming to see him. He was a fine-looking man, my grandfather. Back in the day he was.

As I cinched my tie I thought about my date waiting out in the car. How she looked like Cleopatra in her Egyptian-style makeup, velvet dress, brown feet, and cumulus waves of hair. I thought about how she was sucking down the beers and smoking my cigarettes; how she might have opened the car door and planted her feet in the cool grass. She was part Sioux on her father's side. He was a colonel in the army and he told me he had seen a Sasquatch when he was a boy living in Arkansas. He and his family were on a road trip when he saw it lumber across the road behind them. He said he had never told his parents. I searched his face for lies and came up empty eyed. I could see his Sioux heritage in his face. His daughter had it less so, but enough to where she darkened into a soft leather-red throughout the summer months, when it was easy to believe she was a full-blood who happened to wear a lot of makeup. Then winter came and the sun slipped down the sky and so did her color. I could see the Anglo in her then. Her mother's side, mostly.

I remember going to her house on the night of the dance. I was early and despite her instructions to have me wait upstairs, her father showed me downstairs, where she was sitting at her mirror, about to put on her make-up. That was the first time I saw her without her face and I was stunned by the simple elegance of her beauty. My friends would often joke about her use of makeup, call her "cake-face," but I had seen the face beneath the face. Not to mention the indisputable fact that they not so secretly coveted her and would have bedded her gleefully if given the chance.

What did I care? Fine may be the line between Egyptian whore and queen. And she was mine and she was going to drink all the beer if I didn't extract myself from the hospital room. My grandfather was sitting up in his bed and I sat next to him and told him I had to go. That was over a quarter century ago and I don't remember what all was said. But my body remembers leaning in and hugging him. He still had some flesh on him and I could feel its softness through his hospital gown. More sour than sweet, his aftershave from a few days before still clung to his cheeks and neck. "I've got to go, grandpa." Then he said something that must have been very sweet and final because I put my chin on his shoulder and cried for a couple of minutes, which was a long time under the circumstances.

Lately my own father tells me he has about ten more years of life, give or take. This is how he prepares to let go. This is how he tries to control what cannot be controlled. And yet the first death we die is just as often not the death of our parents. When I was about sixteen my father alerted me to this imminent outcome. I remember it so viv-idly because I was tripping on acid. My friend Dilson and I had shared a hit and then hiked to first falls above Bell Canyon Reservoir, where we stayed until dusk. When I got home that evening, I was good-tired from a full day of sunning and swimming in the late summer snow-melt that had collected in the reservoir. I preferred wilderness to any other place, especially when I felt vulnerable. Other kids made plans to go to the movies or to the football game. I made plans to relinquish myself to chemicals and to the ensuing madness.

On one of the few days I actually went to high school, I looked out the bus window and saw my friend stumbling out into the field with a can of gasoline and an old blanket. I found out later that he had sat under that blanket for half the day and sniffed gasoline. Like everyone else I knew, except perhaps the Mormon kids who smiled like they knew it all, he was lost. Then one night he dropped three hits and found a mighty luminous Jesus floating in the foothills above his house with its long driveway on the east side of town. I did not begrudge him. Who in hell was I to tell him how to find a foothold in the world, even if it meant clinging to the unreal, something more ethereal than a cloud? I had already wandered so far into the labyrinth that it would take until this very moment to find my way out.

The night my father told me he would die someday, he was wait-ing up for me, which is what he did whenever he came to visit. I don't know why his death hadn't occurred to me sooner. Perhaps it was because of my total devotion to the moment, the hour, the day, the week, but not the month or the year, which were too distant. But the more he explained, the further I buried my face into the warmth of his chest. He rubbed my back and said that this wouldn't happen for many years. Nothing to worry about right now. Nothing to worry about ever. My eyes were closed, but I still kept seeing. I felt a strange welling heat, as if I were exempt from natural law and even though my father would die, I myself was deathless and moments away from subduing the world with my beauty.

★ ★ ★

Rather than fret about what has faded and what will end, I work out in the yard with Wilder. I prepare the garden plot and he sits in the flowerbed and grows. He is all possibility and becoming. I break the soil, pull the weeds, and stack the stones. I notice how the sow bugs and the sow bug killers live together beneath the rotted leaves. I curse the sparrows for dumping their dead chicks in the garden, where the ants have at them.

By evening, my fingers ache and curl shut from grasping tools and I am ready to be done. If Wilder could ignore the darkness and the cool of night, he would curl up like a pill bug and go to sleep right here if I let him. But I get him into the house, cleaned up, and fed. I help him with his jammies and then we sit in bed with the windows open. The room is bathed in the cool blue light of sundown in the West and the breeze carries news of the world: the deep smell of heat leaving the grass and the fermenting rot of last year's apples, every last one pierced with the bore holes of moths. I hear the robins calling to one another in the dark. The smells and sounds and memories of my boyhood drift into the house. *Hello* and *goodbye*, I say as they carry off small pieces of my life. Then I kill a mosquito so it cannot feed on my son while he is sleeping.

My grandfather used to say that at twenty, a man wants a good lay; at forty he wants a good steak; and at sixty, he wants a good shit. What about at eighty, grandpa? What does a man want then? My grandpa is dead, so I will put these true words in his mouth: *What does a man want at eighty? Depends,* he says, *on many things.* Dead grandpa knows more than living grandpa, but I won't press him for more details. When the time comes, I will find out for myself and then, many years later, long after I am dead, my own son or his son will come looking for me for answers I will not give, either.

For now it feels good just to rest my tired bones atop the cool sheets. I turn on the television and surf until I see a little girl in the hospital. She doesn't look well: her skin is much too pale and the lamps of her eyes are turned too low. I glance at Wilder. He is watching intently with his chin on his chest. His concentration makes me nervous so I change the channel then change it back when he protests. I wonder how much a three-year-old can understand. I would ask Kim, but she is taking a shower and I don't know if I can get up anyway.

The little girl is having her picture taken with some of the nurses. Apparently she is about to go home and I tell Wilder as much. "Look at all the balloons," I say, pointing. The little girl begins to cry as she moves from nurse to nurse, hugging them around the waist, thanking and telling them how much she will miss them. But then as the narrative progresses, we learn that the little girl has terminal cancer and that she is going home to die. There is nothing more the doctors can do, the female voice-over explains.

This story fattens my dread and before I know it I'm tearing up. I'm careful not to make any noise, though, because I don't want to upset Wilder. Too late. Wilder is already crying. Rather than shushing him or telling him some lie, I put my hand behind his head and let the experience run its course because I don't know what else to do. A couple of minutes later Kim comes into the room, takes one look at me and Wilder, then at the television, then back at me. "Are you okay? What's wrong?" she asks, drying her hair with a towel.

I distract Wilder by asking him if he wants a fruit bar. And thus begins his problems with food or, as my brother Christian calls it, emotional eating. Then I change the channel. "I'll tell you later," I whisper to Kim. I am certain that Wilder didn't understand that the little girl was going to die. All he knew was that she was sad and that made him sad. Children are so sweet and kind, it is hard to think they will become adults. When a child dies, it is like a quiet implosion, a white-hot blast that scorches everything around it. I would wager that the death of a child was the inspiration for the atomic bomb.

★ ★ ★

The sun goes up and down and up again. Wilder and I resume our daily walks. Our route loops past Mill Creek, circles around, and concludes in the cemetery, the place of conclusion. Apart from the groundskeepers and visitors, Wilder and I usually have the place to ourselves. We both consider the cemetery one of the highlights of our walk. I wouldn't say it is a very beautiful place, but it is safer than walking the road.

The road we take into the neighborhood parallels the cemetery and functions as a throughway for the south wind. Wilder stops and turns his back to it. He tells me he can't breathe. I squat and close his jacket. "Watch me," I say, facing the wind and taking long, deep breaths. "See, you can breathe. It just seems like you can't." I must have been persuasive because then Wilder turns around and we continue our walk. Once we get off Honeycutt Street the wind dies and Wilder lets go of my hand and runs ahead.

As he gets farther and farther away, I cannot escape the metaphorical gleam of the moment. If each day he runs a little farther, how long will it take before he disappears completely? That is what children do:

they disappear. So I do what I can to memorize Wilder's beauty. The softness of his chubby little hands and gold-blond hair; the directness of his words and how quickly he forgives. Given his curiosity, whenever we enter the cemetery I wonder what he is going to ask me and if I will be able to answer him.

A few days ago we saw people gathered around a freshly filled grave. They were laughing deep belly laughs and carrying on while the children released balloons and swung from the canopy above the grave. Music came from a pickup with its door open.

"What are they doing?" Wilder asked.

"It looks like they're celebrating. They're having a party."

Wilder looked up at me and squinted: "A birfday party?"

"No, just a party."

"Otay," he said.

"Okay."

Wilder and I were both a little surprised by the display. Perhaps in accordance with the sign that says the cemetery is a sacred place, and which asks that visitors therefore refrain from playing games or picnicking, the people we have seen here are generally sedate and inconspicuous. In fact, they are usually so quiet, I barely notice them. But the revelers don't give me the choice of whether or not to notice them. Where once I was a kind of satellite, remote, mute, and watchful, I was now a distant participant. I was not quite the silent watcher standing in the dark beneath my neighbor's tree. I was real. I wondered, What do these people have for me?

Wilder had the luxury of having other things on his mind. The cemetery had piled mountains of dirt on the southeast corner of the property. Once we had squeezed through the gate, it was a short walk to the mounds and Wilder headed right for them. "I'll follow you," I said as I watched a small group of cedar waxwings sit in the branches. They reminded me of punk rockers with their painted faces and crests that resemble Mohawks.

When we reached the top of the highest mound, Wilder slid down the other side. I was about to join him when I saw a bone sticking out of the dirt. I squatted and pulled it out of the soil. It was an ulna. That it belonged to a human was supported by what appeared to be fragments of a wooden coffin.

"Come down here, Daddy," Wilder insisted.

"I'm on my way." I slipped the bone and a piece of the coffin in my back pocket and down I went. Wilder wasn't ready to leave the mounds, though, and as he dilly-dallied I divided my time between looking out for him and watching an elderly man care for a grave. Down on one knee, he used hand shears to clip the overgrown grass. Then he took a small brush from his back pocket and swept the clippings and dirt that had gathered in the inscription. When his work was done, he stood, tilted his head, and looked at the grave for a minute or so. Then he eased into his car and drove away.

I finally convinced Wilder to continue our walk. Once he joined me at the foot of the mound, I brushed off his pants and looked him over. It is tiresome, but I don't trust dirt, snow, and grass. Nor anything else that conceals. No pant tears or blood flowers. Everything was fine, so I pointed him down the road and off he went. Now that the elderly man was out of sight, I walked over to investigate the grave. Judging by the names and dates, the grave must have belonged to the man and his deceased wife. Her inscription was complete, but his bore only his name and the date of his birth followed by a hyphen. Trilliums lined the top of the grave. Something had been eating their leaves. I do not care to have my name etched in stone while I am alive.

Wilder was circling the trunk of an enormous blue spruce, perhaps the oldest tree here. He called it his tree. I left the road, crossed the grass, and walked toward him. The stones were slick and I worried that Wilder would slip, fall, and hit his head. I'm exhausted by fear. By the time I got there, Wilder had already devised a game for us to play. We were Cooper's hawks, and my nest was on one side of the tree and his was on the other. I settled into the nest that Wilder had imagined for me. At my feet were some very old gravestones, some dating back to the mid-nineteenth century.

I found myself subtracting and figuring out how long it had been since these people had died: Eighty years ago, one hundred years ago, one hundred and twenty years ago. Apart from the wars, back then it must have felt like we still had a chance. On bad days, or whenever I think about all that we have done to our planet, to ourselves, and to each other, I look into people's faces and into the sky and it feels like the world is on the threshold of some imminent disaster. At times like these, all I want to do is apologize to my children.

The sky started to cloud up and the whole place turned gray. I told Wilder that he had a couple more minutes to play before we had to head back. I didn't want to get stuck out there in a lightning storm. When the minutes passed and Wilder was still not ready, I talked to him about the lightning and how it could hurt us and he snapped out of his play world and joined me in my fear. He looked worried so I told him it was okay but that we needed to start walking home. Up ahead I saw a worker packing a newly filled grave.

When we reached him he had turned off the machine and was preparing to cover the grave with sod. *Green sod above lie light, lie light. Good night, dear heart, good night, good night.*

"How are you doing?" I asked as Wilder and I approached him.

"I'm doing alright," he said, under his green ball cap. His soul patch and lower lip covered a knot of chew.

"I found something that might interest you." I reached around and took the bone and the coffin fragment from my back pocket. I felt like I had found him out, or that I was accusing him of a crime. As he took off his gloves and stuffed them in his overalls, I entertained the idea and went so far as to imagine reporting the incident to the local news station. Maybe they'd interview me and Wilder and ask us some stupid question like, *When you woke up today, did you think you would find a human bone?* Wilder would look up at me for some help finding the words and I'd smile at him and then I'd say to the reporter, *Well, yes. Didn't everyone?* The fact was I didn't feel a thing for that bone.

"What you got there?" he asked, taking the bone in one hand and the coffin fragment in the other. The worker was just a kid, so I remembered not to act deferentially.

"I found it in the dirt over there," I said, using my thumb to point behind me.

The kid nodded. "That's crazy," he said, turning over the ulna and studying it.

I asked him where they got the dirt and he told me they got it from the oldest part of the cemetery.

"We're expanding it," he said, using his thumb to scrape mud from the bone. "That's crazy," he said again, clearly at a loss for words.

"You ready to get going?" I asked Wilder. He didn't take his eyes off the kid.

"Yes," he said.

"Okay, let's go. Take it easy," I said, glancing at the kid.

"Tated easy," Wilder repeated.

We cut across the lawn to the fence. The worker had since been joined by a man in a flatbed truck with a pulley system used for conveying and lowering headstones. The kid handed him the bone. Then he motioned toward me discreetly. The man saw me watching them. He put the truck in park and it rolled forward a little. Then he said something and the kid spat, put on his gloves, and laughed.

★ ★ ★

One night before we fall asleep, in the event I do not put down this wish in writing, I make Kim promise not to bury me. I will burn and rise in embers and in crackling bits of ash.

★ ★ ★

Today it is snowing late spring snow. Gray and wet, the weather doesn't change how I feel when I look north across the street at my neighbors' house. A young married couple lives there. They might be in their middle twenties. They welcomed us into the neighborhood with creamed honey and a warm loaf of homemade bread. Five minutes later, Wilder's face was aglow. Honey and its pleasures are very old and the Mormon Church has learned to tap this primal heritage. I wonder how many wars have been averted, how many people have been led and misled by a jar of honey.

When Greer was born, the kids across the street brought over a gift basket with a candle, some cookies, and a tiny stuffed lamb. I told my friend Metcalf that eating lamb is like eating the loins of angels. "Angel loins are better," he said. "Trust me." Metcalf is fighting prostate cancer, so his words have a certain pull or gravity when it comes to saying what is good and beautiful. Evenings when I've watched the sun pull its sheet of light out of the grass or across the stones in the field, I've thought, *Look at the heaviness.* That is the way it is with Metcalf. His face is that field and his words are those stones. He says he does not recognize the landscape of his own body. Something similar is happening with those kids across the street.

I rise hours before the sun, and so most mornings I watch the young man leave for work in the dark. His lights slash across my window and I wonder if he sees me in here, sitting at this table, watching him. I don't see her as much. When I do, it is usually not until late in the day, when the starlings fill the trees, the robins start singing again, and Kim, Greer, Wilder, and I have returned from our evening walk. She looks different to me. Her hair and her body. The way she moves. Some days I have to look at her twice to recognize her. The wind blows her hair across her face and she doesn't stop it, which tells me something.

But today there is no wind. Blue sky and a high sun. She waits on the stoop in her Sunday best while he locks the door. His tie is pink and fat and friendly. Then he puts his hand on the small of her back and guides her down the stairs and to the car. Maybe I would take comfort in religion if I were someone else, someone with the stones to believe in something so improbable. Even then I am not sure it would really change anything. However disagreeable, however ghostly and mysterious, facts are still the nails that hold together the world. Facts are born but they do not die, exactly. They are what move the rocking chair in the empty room. They are the whisper of my name when I am alone. Once facts move into a house, they cannot be driven out. It's as good as theirs. They are immune to their own poison.

★ ★ ★

I had a friend named Tosser who had a permed Mo-flop (an unspiked Mohawk), wore purple Converse, boasted an enormous

Goody comb, and wore jeans that were so tight, his package had no choice but to bunch to one side. He was a little guy with a hefty moose knuckle, which he proudly displayed, apparently for the benefit of any girl who he could lure back to his house. Once there he would seduce them with a back massage on his water bed, back when water beds were exotic. I remember partying at his house one night and passing his room and seeing one of his captures. Perhaps because of the alcohol or cocaine or whatever Tosser was using and sharing at the time, the girl's features were lazy and off, and when she looked at me I could not tell if she were resigned or pleading.

Tosser was a messed-up kid, but he had his reasons. His older sister—a pretty girl with perfect teeth and Farrah Fawcett–style hair—overdosed on aspirin. Her story is strangely typical, stupid, and tragic in that way that only a teenage love story can be. After her parents refused to let her go to the lake with her boyfriend, I'm guessing she gobbled the pills to get back at them and because she honestly believed her life was over. But then she realized her mistake, got scared, and told her parents, who rushed her to the emergency room. Doctors looked her over. Listened to her heart. Did not joke about it being broken. Ran some tests. And sent her home. She hadn't been home for ten minutes when she became violently ill. Again her parents rushed her to the hospital. She died in the parking lot.

True story. I've known it since I was fifteen. Over the last twenty-five years, I've spent a few idle moments wondering about the dead and what else they might have become had their circumstances or luck been different. To this day I'll pass them on the road. Just last week I saw Kim's grandmother, Lita. She sat so low beneath the steering wheel I could barely see her. But she clearly had somewhere to go. The dead I know seem busy and a little worried, like they are always watching a blue sky and preparing for a storm they know is coming. The dead are like us in that they cannot stop moving if they want to survive. Rarely are the dead ever just that. We see them in the night sky and in our dreams and in the living faces of other people, and in this complicated way the dead live on and have lives of their own.

I was twenty the year the eighteen-year-old son of my mother's childhood friend chose a balmy autumn day to hike into the rolling and heavily flowered foothills above Salt Lake City and put a bullet through his head. When a neighbor heard the news, she confided to my mother's friend that she had seen the boy walking up the driveway and that he had smiled at her even though in reality he was already dead. When and where suicides shoot themselves matters because it tells everyone who loved them how badly they wanted to die. Those who kill themselves after making love on a summer night, or lying in the shade of a cherry tree, or standing within view of the ocean know this better than anyone.

But Tosser's sister's death was not that kind. There was nothing remotely beautiful about her death, or if there was, it escapes me. I saw her once in life and the other times were in photographs. Back then I would have never guessed she was entirely gone by how her memory had settled like dust in the rooms and in the words that were spoken in the rooms with the doors closed.

Long after a child has died, parents will still carry the death. Elephants use their trunks and gorillas use their hands. Maybe humans did so, too, at one time, but now we carry death and the unspeakable in our faces. I can still remember the defeat on Tosser's mother's face. How each line and pore was saturated with loss. Retinol in reverse. I can see her at the kitchen table with a glass of wine that trembles as she taps it with her fingernails, which were always clean and painted.

They kept a caged parrot in the front room and sometimes late at night it spoke the girl's name. The otherwise clean house smelled sour and stank of droppings. And the dogs were kept in a cage in the backyard. One day I forgot myself and told Tosser how fucked up it was to keep those dogs caged up like that, not realizing, of course, that he was also in a cage that held him wherever he went. His face turned pale and he started shaking, which was how his frail body had come to express fury. It was as if he realized that his reasons were not reasons, but he was still forced to act on them. Then he kicked me out. If I were to walk into that house today, I would know I was walking into aftermath. I didn't think much then about other people's loss. Apparently that part of my brain was sleeping and I did almost everything I could to ensure it didn't awaken. I didn't understand how some people could wake up every day feeling sorry they had.

But even I know that loss is what gives life its edge, and that sometimes it cuts so deeply the hemorrhaging cannot be stopped. This wound can be simulated by imagining one's house burning or in ashes. What can I save? What do I do? Run inside the swirling orange-blue strangeness? The mesmerizing, killer tongues of flame? I think I would stand there, naked, shivering, waiting for someone to give me something hot to drink and put a blanket around me. Minutes would go by and everything would still be smoldering. Whereas before I would not notice my nakedness, I would start to. I would look over my left shoulder and then my right and see the streets were filled with naked people just like me, standing in front of their houses, which were also afire, all waiting for blankets.

★ ★ ★

When my neighbors get back from church, Wilder and I are out front raking up pine needles beneath our enormous blue spruce. The tree was planted circa 1952, or around the time our house was built. Kim tells me the tree is ugly and she wants it down. She knows that the tree's appearance is arguable, so she appeals to my protectiveness and adds that she is afraid it will blow over some night in a storm and crush us in our sleep. I admit it is a powerful image. But I can't bring myself to fell the old tree, which so far has withstood decades of wind and rain and people's ill-intentions. I wave hello to my neighbors. There is maybe thirty feet between us, but it feels much farther. He nods and she smiles and waves. Wilder sees me wave and he calls out to them. They wave again. I get anxious thinking about sitting in church. I've only been twice that I remember, and not by choice.

I went when I was maybe five years old and visiting my grandparents in Idaho Falls. The second time I went I was about twelve and staying with my childhood friend, "P." "P" was the first letter of his middle name and "P" cried funny and wiped boogers on his bedroom wall. I thought it was a shame because his mother had spent hours redoing his room and had just put up expensive wallpaper with a horn, sword, and drum pattern and here he was, unapologetically collecting boogers. He would line them up like cars in a junkyard.

We were going to the lake on Monday, so I spent the weekend at his house and that included Sunday. When I walked into the church, I felt people trying not to look at me. "P" had been raised a "good" Mormon, but he did the same shit we all did and plus he nearly drowned me at the lake. We had used floating devices to swim out to a little island some three hundred yards away from the boat. We tried to stone a jackrabbit as it nibbled on a sagebrush. I made the point that his aim was terrible and he took both the floating devices and swam away.

I swam after him, pleading for him to stop. He just kept going. When I was a kid living in Maine, I had taken swimming lessons and had earned pollywog status, which meant I could do the dog paddle and float on my back when I needed to rest, so that is what I did to stay alive. I told his mom when I got back to the boat and she took him by the arm and, using words that seldom cross a good Mormon's lips, gave him a tongue-lashing that made him cry.

Each year, magpies nest in the branches and scrub jays cache peanuts in the loose dirt beneath the old blue spruce. Wilder finds a few the rake has turned up and he reburies them. The neighbors have gone inside. Were it not for the scheme of things, my habit of watching them might seem an odd business. We are partly defined by what we notice, after all, and usually I don't like what I see. But every so often I see something tender. I watched the neighbors grow their baby. Granted I caught glimpses. In contrast to the gaze, glimpses are naturally incisive. And these were beautiful and enough to remind Kim and me of the experience we had conceiving, growing, and birthing Wilder and, later, Greer.

Looking at my children, it is sometimes hard to get back to those early experiences. Wilder's sweet voice will thin out and Greer's fat little cheeks with smooth away like butter on a hot griddle. Watching the neighbor grow her child was a way to remember, but it was also a way to let go. We were done making children. So I became a witness to the personal lives of these strangers.

I saw her the day she went into the hospital. She was so big that she waddled like a woman with an enormous baby inside of her; like a woman who was cradling a boulder. "My back hurts just looking at her," Kim laughed, thankful that she got nowhere near as big. The husband is scrambling to finish loading the car before his wife gets there. It all comes back to me. By the time she is ready to load up, he has made two trips into the house and gathered all of their things. She puts her arm over his shoulder and he slides under her and hoists her into the car. He has mythical, golden hair, those loose curls that resemble pencil shavings. Women often give birth at home with the help of a midwife, but Kim and I agreed that would involve taking unnecessary risks: if something went wrong, we reasoned, the doctors and their machines could help us.

Most of the men I know have found the births of their children to be among their most stressful experiences. But when compared to the stress their wives must endure, men generally do not feel comfortable voicing their feelings. Nor is American culture very helpful when it comes to addressing the man's experience of childbirth. Either he is horrified by the baby's exit or he passes out or experiences a kind of birth himself, whereby he is suddenly awakened to the "miracle" of life. None of these extremes describes my experience. I cried each time one of my children was born, which in itself is not unusual. But understanding why I cried is a complicated matter. I know there are several reasons, including that life as I had known it for thirty-six years had ended. But if I had to give one reason—if I had to embody it—I would start by looking at Kim.

The word "labor" does not describe what I saw. When I think of labor, I think of a man with a shovel. He digs a little bit, wipes his brow, spits, and leans on his tool. With Kim it was as if every part of her body shared the burden of readying Wilder for his grand entrance into the world: toes grasping; back arching; skin glistening; chest rising and falling, rising and falling; eyes closing with each wave of contractions. I did what I could by rubbing her back and shoulders, but in the throes of such intense pain, if I were not touching her, I doubt she would know I was there. Pain obliterates and this exclusion was portentous.

Still, despite my dreams of leaving the life I helped create, I have had to give up very little since the birth of our children. Perhaps some men view their decision to become fathers as a sacrifice, and it is, but I chose fatherhood, although I am not always sure what that means. I know I could be doing other things, living other lives, but I wonder if these are not moot notions. However much it might seem otherwise, our lives are finite and so, too, are the lives we would otherwise be living. After a certain point, even the variations of our dreams merge into a single theme.

Hour twenty came and the doctor knelt down and put her hand inside of Kim. "Okay, there's his head," she said. Wilder was there, but he was not there. The doctor had reached into a hidden dimension and touched what Kim and I had only thought of touching. Going on twenty-seven hours without sleep, I was a wreck. I looked at Kim, though, and saw none of my fading. She sat straight and had a look of resolve I had never seen. I felt reassured, but watching her endure the intense pain of labor was almost unbearable. Knowing that whatever entered her bloodstream would also enter Wilder's, Kim was committed to giving birth naturally, without the aid of painkillers. She drew the line at twenty hours and requested an epidural.

Within minutes a doctor wheeled in a small metal table that held the instruments needed for the procedure. I decided that I would watch to make sure nothing went wrong. Then I naively wondered if by watching I might place undue pressure on the doctor, which might undermine her concentration and cause her to slip. *You're being absurd,* I thought to myself. The doctor opened Kim's gown, revealing her lovely back. "Stay very still," she said as she readied the needle.

The needle itself was six inches long and thick as far as needles go: it had to penetrate between the vertebrae and into the epidural space, which is filled with cerebrospinal fluid. It was difficult, but I forced myself to watch until the instant before the needle touched her skin. A few minutes later, Kim was numb from the waist down. Now that she was no longer in pain, the mood improved, but her contractions—their frequency and duration—did not. That is why we decided not to wait any longer and deliver by cesarean, a procedure with a long and brutal history. For over four hundred years, or up until the mid-nineteenth century, it was used only when the mother was dead or dying.

The nurse wheeled Kim into the operating room to prepare her for the procedure. I was instructed to don a gown, hat, and booties before entering the OR. I did so hurriedly and then joined Kim, who had now been prepped and draped with dark blue sheets. She reminded me of an installation piece. Had she delivered vaginally, I may have worked up the nerve to watch Wilder arrive. But the cesarean changed that and I opted instead to stand by Kim's head, where we could reassure each other.

The doctors moved quickly and methodically and within minutes Wilder was out in the air, shining and grunting. Today he has golden auburn hair with streaks of blond highlights most women would pay hundreds for, so it is hard to believe that his hair was originally thick and black. Most striking was the deep purple-blue color of his skin; the color of the body before it breathes.

I did not go to him right away. I stayed with Kim and stroked her face as I talked to her. I lingered at the threshold of our new and unfamiliar life, perhaps sensing that these would be some of the last moments we would spend alone for a while. Finally one of the doctors called me over. "Go meet your son," Kim said.

I had to walk past the drape that concealed her lower body and when I did I saw the violent smile in her lower abdomen. Wilder was lying in a white towel, crying softly and squirming. The doctor carefully cleared his mouth and wiped away gelatinous bits of blood from his face and chest. I held his hand and felt jelly in his palm. "It's nice to meet you," I said. Behind us the needle swam in and out of Kim's body. Time to close the confidential envelope. Velvet jewel bag. Door to the room with no windows. I turned and looked at her. Her eyes were closed. Safe at last.

★ ★ ★

Last summer my father and his girlfriend, Lisa, visited from Maine and together with my brother we hiked up the mountain to Bell Canyon Reservoir. I hadn't been there for twenty years, or since I was about twenty, and I was sure it would be gone. My boyhood friend Brody used to live near the trailhead, and as we neared the area I searched for his old house among the high gables, exotic trees, and terraced yards. I knew it was somewhere in the mess of development, but I could not find it on the side of the mountain because the mountainside was gone, cleaved away and trucked off to the landfill, where it would be used to bury our garbage.

I haven't seen Brody since I was about nineteen. I used to hear about him from time to time. Rumor had it he went to prison. For all I know, he may be there now. The last time I saw him, it seemed like he was still about fifteen years old, the result, I guessed, of his prolonged drug and alcohol abuse. My own brain cells have always been too happy to luxuriate in synthetics. I shudder when I think of the damage I might have done.

I used to dream about Brody, and at one point I was convinced he was in trouble so I set out to find him. I did and he was, but there was nothing I could do for him. Was I thinking I could change his desire for darkness? A mutual friend had told me where he worked, so I reluctantly drove up to Silver City. I thought back to the night when I was drinking and shooting pool at a local bar on Main Street. I was with a group of beautiful girls I knew from college and we were playing a couple local drunks and winning. One of the men looked at me and said, "I used to know a guy like you. He got raped." My mother has always said nothing good ever comes from alcohol. I am hard pressed to think of an exception.

When I found Brody, he was just finishing his shift, and we sat and drank beer and picked over the shitty finger foods the bar sets out during happy hour. That was before I was much of a drinker. I sipped a beer and told him about my dreams and why I thought I was having them. He didn't say anything, but when he smiled his eyes narrowed and the drug rash around his mouth cracked and began to bleed. He was a very long way from the kid whose house was high on the hill. Including the views, he seemed to have had every advantage.

I looked out across the reservoir as I waited for my brother, father, and Lisa to catch up. The surface was smooth and still until a cruising cutthroat trout took a fly and made ripples. It was hard not to look around and remember, and not to feel events and experiences that happened over a quarter-century ago, when I was still new at life. I cannot resist the presence of the past. But I try not to hang on to it, because if I did, it would be the end of me. I just let it flow over me like wind or something that cannot be held or kept.

The opposite is true with respect to my children. As much as I would sometimes like to do otherwise, I cannot let go. And maybe this will be enough to save us. I have less time than my parents, who had their children young, so I tell myself I must make the days count. My father calls to me and I lift a hand. I cannot hear him breathing. He's in good shape for a man his age. White hair and bronze-red face. He is moving slowly, but he is here, in the mountains, as is my brother who, like me, hasn't hiked up here since he was a kid.

I don't remember ever seeing my brother so animated. And then I realize that I don't know him now, and that he is giving himself to the moment and to the past and to his memories; to a time when all our lives could have become anything we chose. My father says that my brother is the only person he knows who has learned to stop time. I do my fair share of looking back and of wishing. But my kids keep me from getting stuck. I try to avoid the old songs and places. When I do go back the way I came, sometimes it is for want of an earlier time in my life. But really it is because I want to stop time like my brother. And why wouldn't I when I have more days behind me than I have ahead?

A few months after Wilder was born, I told my father that in some ways I understood him more, but that in other ways I understood him less. "You'll have to explain what you mean sometime," he said. But we both know we won't broach the subject again.

"Coming here was a good idea," my father says, clutching my shoulder. His shirt is off and I see my own body twenty-eight years from now. I could do worse. I wonder how Wilder and Greer will look at me when I am older. I hope they don't feel sorry for me, but they probably will. It has been hard watching my parents get old. There is something pathetic about aging. Something frail and mean, obscene and sad in a way that nothing else can be.

Now that they are in their final decades of life, they seem to have mostly forgotten the challenges of child-rearing. They know that life changes once children are born and that it is hard, but for them this difficulty is an idea and not a palpable intensity that informs every aspect of life. They cannot understand my peculiar sense of dread because we are from and living in different times. They are thinking about themselves, after all, about who will care for them and how it will feel as they get closer to the end.

★ ★ ★

After my grandfather died, we all thought my grandmother would be quick to follow. But as the months went by and my grandmother continued to deplete her children's inheritance, sympathy waned. "Why doesn't she let go and die with some dignity?" we would ask. I would not figure out the answer to this question until a few months ago, when Kim's grandmother, Lita, died. She was ninety-six and had spent the majority of her working life sewing garments for the Mormon Church. When she could no longer work—her vision poor and her hands wrecked and rendered claws by arthritis—the church paid her pennies a day for retirement.

I once made the comment to Kim that all Lita did was eat, sleep, shit, and watch Lawrence Welk. "What kind of life is that?" I would ask. Now that she's gone and I myself have grown older, I realize that what I saw as evidence of a pointless life was actually a complex of the most pleasurable things a body can do. Kim and I saw her the night she died. Her room was just off the kitchen at Kim's parents' house. The door was open and she was sleeping the sleep of the final dream. Her breathing was shallow and labored and impossible to ignore. The pauses between breaths were so long, I thought she was going to die before dessert. Maybe we would see her spirit rise, blinking, bewildered, and finally free from the corporeal fog and itch of morphine.

Kim, a natural-born logician, would have the gumption to open the window. And with a little help from Kim's dad and a broom, Lita would be shooed out and into the winter air. "I think she is going to die tonight," Kim's mom said. And she did, not long after Kim and I had left.

I was wrong to think that a body could quit life so easily. With or without some sense of what awaits us, under most circumstances we cling to life as long as we can. I know people who professed the solace of religion, but they, too, were weak-kneed and trembling on the threshold. I want to be full of desire.

★ ★ ★

My life is a long road with aging parents on one end and children on the other. Without saying so, my parents want me to know time is running out, and I get the feeling that every word, no matter how wrong, is precious. At this point the key is to keep the words simple. Then my mother says that Kim and I should not be so overly protective. That we should do this and not do that. I listen politely most of the time. But inside I'm wishing she and my father would remember what it was like to have small children, and to consider what it means to have brought children into the world at this point in history. It probably doesn't matter, but I ask them if the world were the same place when I was a kid. They say, *Well, no,* to which I respond, *I didn't think so.*

For their part, Wilder and Greer expect me to be a child again. It's hard on my back. They are lovely kids and they look and smell so sweet I suspect they are really a kind of flower in disguise. And Kim?

She wants what I want: a safe world and a healthy planet. Something to hope for. And, in Kim's words, "a full night's sleep without being sucked on." Plus a massage and her old body back. She is supple and lovely and the softness of her skin is second only to Greer's. She looks at me as if she doesn't quite believe me, and then says, "I guess that says something for a body that has been on lease for the last four years." When I check on her each morning, I notice how tired and troubled her face looks when she sleeps. I realize how hard she works and it fills me with admiration and sadness.

Nurturing relationships is work and loving the people in our lives is not automatic. I don't know that I will ever love people the way I imagine I could. I'm slowly filling the hole love digs for me, one shovel-load at a time. I flush when people talk about family values or God and His love as if they and He and It were as static and immutable as a kitchen table around which nothing of any substance is said.

I want to see well and truly, but it might be too painful. My father says we haven't made any new memories since 1994 when we visited his older brother Herbert in Spain. They hadn't seen each other in over forty years, and when they did they each spoke the other's name and then hugged and cried. My father is right: we haven't made any new memories. But my father and I had our chance. Now I am here and he is there. I am this other person with children who will one day not have time for me, and all there will be left to do is learn to love the shadows of those I love, and to salvage the old memories. In retrospect, the stages of life appear as subterfuge.

★ ★ ★

When my father looks into his girlfriend's eyes he is seeing a memory. They knew each other when I was a kid and we were all still living

in Maine. My father and his girlfriend worked with mentally chal-
lenged kids. My brother Christian and I used to go to work with him
and play with the kids there and they were some of the finest human
beings I have ever met. What could I accomplish with an army of
those beautiful and broken kids, many of whom would not live to see
their thirtieth birthday? I am thinking specifically of Carol and the
perpetually childlike, sweet dopiness of his Down's Syndrome face.
Despite his size and strength, he treated me and my brother with great
care and tenderness. He was like that gorilla with the kitten. He died
when he was twenty-four. *Sorry, Carol, but I needed to wake you for a
moment. Go back to sleep, please.*

Each year my father and his colleagues would orchestrate various
wilderness outings for the kids and I was always eager to join them.
One summer we drove to an A-frame deep in the hills and the kids
wandered around touching the trees and the plants as if they were
the most precious things. Carol got stung by a bee and charged down
the path, screaming and moaning like a great, hairless bear. Of course
we did not know he had been stung by a bee and my brother and I
thought for sure the scale in his head had finally tipped and that he
was going to kill us.

In the end, we just stepped aside and he ran past us down the trail
and out of sight. That night we made a bonfire and sang songs to gui-
tars while the adults drank their wine and toked their joints out past
the firelight. The orange light played across the kids' faces, various in
their wonder and novelty, and their eyes were wet from the marriage
of smoke, the night's coolness, and the feeling they were not far from
the ocean.

I insisted on sleeping out by the fire with Carol and one of my
father's colleagues. Late that night a light rain fell and my father

came out, scooped me up, and carried me toward the house. In that euphoric stage between sleep and wakefulness, I could not tell if the *tsst tsst tsst* came from the rain hitting the fire or from the rain hitting me. Inside the adults were sitting around a table drinking coffee and talking loudly. When they saw me they lowered their voices and the pretty ones smiled.

There was a small room off the hallway that smelled like sawdust and wool and my father carried me in there and set me on an old couch he had prepared with blankets and a beautifully treated deer-skin. The window was open a crack and I heard the woodsy sounds and the now-heavy drops of rain striking the leaves. My father kissed me on the head and then left the room and rejoined the adults down the hall. I closed my eyes and buried my face into the skin. Then I slipped into the deep green darkness where everyone was welcoming me back to the fire and they are still.

★ ★ ★

For days neither Kim nor I had seen the neighbors to the north. The curtains were drawn but at night I could see a fissure of light between them. With nothing else to go on, I dismissed the light as precautionary and assumed that mother and child were recovering at the hospital. I joke with Kim that it is my job to notice things and to keep tabs on the neighbors. Although Kim was the first to wonder out loud if something were wrong.

"It's too quiet over there. Too still." Kim stands at the window nursing Greer.

"I haven't seen anybody. Have you?" I ask.

Wilder is out back digging in the flowerbed. I can see him talking to himself as he moves dirt from one place to the other.

"I haven't. Doesn't seem like a place where a new baby lives." Kim's brow furrows.

Now Wilder is using a watering can to add water to the dirt he's piled. Then he puts his hands in it and spreads the mud. Kim joins me at the back door and together we watch Wilder slather his legs in the dark mixture.

"Why don't we get them a little something and walk it over there?" I ask.

Kim opens the back door and tells Wilder not to put the mud in his mouth. "Let's give it a couple days," she said.

The sun sets and rises a couple times and then people dressed in black start showing up at the neighbors' house. Most of them carry flowers. Others bring food. Full-course meals sealed in Tupperware. No toys. Nothing obvious for the baby's room. I haven't seen the neighbors. They must be home, though, because the people stream in and out of the house all day. Kim and I watch this go on and we wonder what has happened.

Eventually Kim talks to the recovering Mormons to the west and they tell her that the baby—a little girl—was born with a massive, inoperable brain tumor. She lived for about two days. Just long enough for the parents to say hello and goodbye, and for the loss to seep into their faces. The next day the young woman's mother spends the entire day on her knees, weeding the flower bed and planting tulips. Beneath religious contradiction, I recognize the need to build and beautify in the wake of loss; and to translate grief into something that outweighs grief. The young woman stays out of sight. The young man comes out into the yard at dusk and plants a tree and ties ribbons in it. For two days the mourners come and go like late-day shadows.

On the morning of the third day I walk to the window, twist open the blinds, and look outside. Cars line my street but no people are about. Soon another car pulls up and parks in front of my house. For a moment I am suspicious and irritated until I see a little boy, dressed in black and holding flowers, emerge from the back seat. Eventually his entire family—two children and two adults, small for a Mormon family—empties out of the car and then walks toward the cemetery. I follow them for a couple of seconds and then my eyes skip ahead, where I see a large group of people just inside the cemetery fence. They are clutching hands and white balloons.

I can see my neighbors standing in the middle of the throng. I put myself there, next to them. I can see the sunlight, tear paths, and a faint haze of perspiration on their faces. Gnats hovering. I lean toward their ears to whisper words of support, but I cannot think of a single word to say. I take a deep breath and smell the turned earth that is hidden beneath a blanket of shiny synthetic turf. The casket is adorable and tragic. And when God's spokesperson steps forward to speak, to translate Its reasons for this waste, will someone please have the decency to place a hand firmly on his shoulder and press a finger to his lips?

PART TWO

HEAT MONSTER

BUT IF ONE OF THE FLAMES, RISING UP IN THE SCHERZO OF FIRE,
TURNED ALL THE WINDOWS BLANK WITH LIGHT, & IF THAT FLAME COULD SPEAK,
AND IF IT SAID TO ME: "YOU LOVED HER, DIDN'T YOU?" I'D ANSWER, HANDS IN MY
POCKETS, "YES." AND THEN I'D LET FIRE AND MISFORTUNE OVERWHELM MY LIFE.
—LARRY LEVIS

Bobby's hair was short and white, as if a light ash had fallen on his head. Nestled in a face of sun-browned skin, his eyes were robin's egg blue and his teeth were large and off-white. Like the rest of us, in the languid summer months he wore cut-off Levis with the slits up the side that revealed his fit, upper thighs. When I was a boy I referred to him as my uncle, but our blood lines began in different places and were thus separated by space and time. He and my father had known each other since they were young men, haunting the Brown Stone stoops of Brooklyn Heights in beach linens and sipping gin from paper bags.

44

Once or twice Bobby drove up to Maine from New York and stayed with us at the house on Sweden Street. He was one of my favorite people because he was always jovial and kind and at my suggestion would leave dollar bills under my pillow. My father, brother, and I in turn visited Bobby several times over the years. The last time was when I was about seventeen and living in Utah. Bobby's apartment is just off Montague Street, which is known for its bars, restaurants, and human traffic. In those days the drinking age was nineteen, so the clerk at the corner store might have done little more than look at me twice before selling me cigarettes and a six-pack of beer, which I would then take to Bobby's apartment and enjoy alone at the kitchen table. The table was positioned near the window and had two chairs, one for Bobby and one for his adopted son, Gordon, a tall, lean, sinewy man with the translucent skin of a night dweller. Pigeons wanted to land on the fire escape, but they would see me and fly away.

Five stories down I could see people doing things people do in the cities. A year older than me, my brother Christian usually spent his days down the street at Bobby's friend Dido's apartment, where he watched David Bowie movies and smoked copious amounts of grass. In the evening he would emerge from Dido's apartment looking very much the polished doll, bleach-blond hair spiked and painted eyes blazing like fires in a dream, and he would stroll down the "Q" like a gorgeous king through the menagerie of brake lights, shadows, and burning cigarettes. Perhaps people thought it was hard for me to live with such a looker, but my brother cast no shadows, and true beauty elevates what lies around it.

While Christian was busy being beautiful, I sat outside the Italian café across the street from Bobby's apartment. Well into the night I watched the women and sometimes the men if I thought I could learn from them. On that particular visit, I was drunk for seven days straight, from sun up to sun down. I wonder what my father thought as he watched me lavish myself in booze. Perhaps he saw himself as a young man and knew that however far I got sucked backward into the alcohol-soaked darkness, at seventeen I was only a hangover and a day-in-the-sun away from rising into a new skin and doing it all over again.

Although he was searching Brooklyn for the desirable elements of his past, he had enough presence of mind to document our trip with at least one black-and-white photograph of me sitting atop Brooklyn Bridge. I'm wearing a dark blue T-shirt with a pocket in the front for my cigarettes, and a pair of Boy Scout pants I got from the second-hand store. The pants are pegged so they would not conceal my signature apparel: a pair of L.L. Bean Canoe Shoes with a hole in each shoe, courtesy of my big toes with their scythe-like nails. Much to the dismay of those around me, after a few months of wearing them without socks, those shoes smelled worse than shit, as if I had strapped two turds on my feet. I tried to disguise the odor, first by spraying the shoes with Lysol, which only made matters worse; and second, by slicking back my hair with fragrant product—a mixture of Colgate shaving cream for scent and egg whites for hold. *Don't smell my shoes! Look at my hair! Isn't it wonderful?*

I'm pinching a cigarette and staring off into the gray distance, just as I was taught to by my father who, even though I had good teeth from braces, is a staunch proponent of the preoccupied and closed-mouthed photograph. He would say, "Look as if you're watching a black curtain of rain sweep across the ocean." My father used relatively complex language to evoke my ponderous expressions, but when my brother is behind the camera he just says, "Okay now, give me 'the look.'"

In addition to being pale from too many overcast days and puffy from the drinking, I was still growing into my head and suffering the loss of the Egyptian. She had left Utah and moved away that year and I was alone and on the rampage. I did not tell my father about my troubles, and I cannot know what difference it would have made if I had. There is only so much the man can do for the boy and the woman for the girl. We have these fissures, though, these hair-thin cracks of light and dark that signal our interiors.

My father has never spoken about certain parts of his past and I suspect he never will. Surely he must know my mother has told me things. Assuming he would rather tell his own story, a few nights ago I called and told him I wanted to create a record of our lives. "What do you want to know?" he asked, and I started by asking him how he met Bobby. What interests me is not that Bobby is twenty years my father's senior, but that he is gay. I could hear my father take a drink of tea and then place the heavy clay mug on the table. "I met him on Fire Island." My father says the island—specifically, Cherry Grove—was once the refuge and playground of the male gay community, but since the '70s, the gays have gradually been replaced by lesbians.

The beach there has the dual distinction of being one of the world's finest as well as the place where the poet Frank O'Hara was struck and killed by a jeep. I don't think they drive jeeps out there anymore unless it is for maintenance, such as emptying trashcans and clearing car-casses that wash ashore. "What were you doing there?" I asked, know-ing I was entering unspoken territory. His throat clearing told me he was uncomfortable. "Terrible nasty things," he said. Torn between respecting his privacy and my need for information, I asked if there was anything else he could tell me. Long pause, then a gulp of tea. "You're going to have to fill in the holes."

Incidentally, I was with my father the last time he visited the island. I was eight or nine. I know we were there in early spring because the beaches were almost empty and the water and the sand were not yet warm to the touch. At one time my father owned his own house on the island, but not anymore and so we stayed in Cherry Grove with Bobby's friend Tony, a body builder and sun worshipper. The big blue veins in his arms wriggled when he did the simplest things, like turn doorknobs and slice tomatoes. Before he tucked me in for the night, my father said he was going out for a while and that he would see me in the morning. I noted the strange smells of the room and the dry sounds of the house and the wet sounds beyond the house that rose out of the ocean.

Then I slept the strange sleep, the one that everybody sleeps several times over the course of one's life, and when I awoke the next morning, I did not know where I was. I looked in the mirror and found a constellation of bug bites on my cheek. I imagined a bug taking a little stroll. After feeding, it cleaned its mouth parts and then shat pin drops of blood. I wanted that bug to experience me killing it one hundred times or something worse, something found in an entomologist's Inferno. I did not like it when things took from me and that has not changed. Unluckily, bugs probably don't feel fear. But daylight had come and my father and I took the boardwalk to the center of the island and got a liverwurst and red onion sandwich wrapped in white waxed paper. The gay islanders were holding a beauty pageant and the contestants strolled across the hotel balcony in lavish gowns and garish makeup. They reminded me of a flotilla of flowers, like those used for a mass burial at sea, or those placed at least once a year in the spot where Frank O'Hara bled into the lion-colored sand.

Later we walked to the outer edge of the island and down the beach. The sky was eggshell white and it is here that my memory of my father begins to fade. *Oh father, father, do you know when you'll die and where you'll go?* I have no doubt that he was there, though, because out of the corner of my eye I can see him holding my shoes. Then I saw her coming. Straight ahead and down the beach fifty yards, she strode toward us, her long, lovely molasses-black legs slashing through the gray air. I studied her as if I were seeing something impossible; a sand hill crane walking across the prairies of the moon. As she drew closer, I saw the suppleness of her thighs and her deep, night-black skin that would have been entire had she not worn a two-piece, hot-pink bikini.

Even as a nine-year-old boy, I was electrified. She advanced across the sand like molten lava, smoldering and cooling there on the edge of the wider world. I imagined climbing her legs. I wanted to lie in her shade, where she would touch my hair and I would read a comic book and savor my favorite candy bar. When we finally passed each other she glanced at me, smiled and said hello to my father. My father then stood very straight, pushed back his shoulders and out his chest, cleared his throat and said hello. Surrounded by the sea of blackness, her white teeth beamed as if her mouth were full of light, and it would be years before I would imagine how her mouth would feel if it covered me.

Of course many years later it would also occur to me that this beautiful creature, this sensuous template upon which I would found my feminine aesthetic, was actually a man striding down the empty beach as if it were a stage made just for him. Still, if she were a man, he walked as beautifully as any woman I have seen or known. In fact, he was one of the most beautiful women I had ever encountered. On the phone the other night, I asked my father if he remembered her and he said he did, vaguely.

So I am essentially alone in this search of mine. My ear is pressed against the earth and I am straining to hear something on the wind. I'm blowing on the coals of the fire my father made over a quarter-century ago. Don't mind me: I'm just trying to make some light to see things by. My father stands in my dreams, watching. He's wearing a pressed shirt and slacks and as usual he can't be a day over twenty. *Are you just going to stand there, or are you going to get down here and help me?* I ask, down on all fours, blowing at the flames. A moth alights on his sleeve and travels down his arm. Its eyes are glowing. He lets it crawl onto his finger and then he blows it into the air as if he is blowing at a match. When he doesn't answer me, I realize the dream has limits, and that hours, days, weeks, months, years, decades of our lives are given no linguistic expression.

The forest is busy at night, he finally says, gazing into the darkness. *Build up the fire.*

★ ★ ★

Kim, Wilder, and Greer are still sleeping and will until the sun rises and soft June light warms the flies and pours through the open window. For now the house is quiet and a cool breeze moves across the floor and over my feet and ankles. It is a mistake to believe that enduring happiness only comes in big doses. I relish the songs of uncommon birds that visit the yard on their way to somewhere near or far, depending on the time of year. Some birds alight in the yard for only a moment. Their stay is so brief; I cannot see enough of them to name. Unnamed birds take up twice the space, which is like never being able to fully catch my breath. Certain species of vireo are so similar, they must be distinguished by noting the color of the underside of their beaks, which are as wide as a wooden match.

I sit in the shade of my trees and witness the honeybees burrowing into the cherry tree blossoms, pollen sacks affixed to their rear legs like golden plates. I am downwind of the rose bush, breathing the heady fragrance and gazing at the mountain's sheer face and cirques filled with late spring snow. Aside from everything else it is, this life is hard and sweet. And yet I still feel as though something is missing. My mother believes this discontent proves the spirit's home is elsewhere. But I know I will never leave the Earth, and so I make a science and an art out of longing.

As a young man, I had not learned to live life on its own terms. I wanted both to live and to escape life. I've always feared death more than life, and without death as an option, I lived and escaped my life with the help of drugs and alcohol. I must have been a child of ten or eleven the first time I smoked grass and gave the void a name. My father, brother, and I were visiting Bobby just after Christmas. A small fire warmed the apartment and the adults laughed while my brother and I pitched pennies against an old trunk.

Bobby stroked his cat as it slept in the windowsill with a holiday ribbon tied around its neck. Now and then the cat would fart and Bobby would wince in disgust. "Well quit petting the fat fucking thing," Dido would laugh under his dark mustache and deep brown skin. He wore camouflage pants and a cable-knit wool sweater that smelled of incense. And when he spoke, his accent was a heavy blend of gay, Puerto Rican, and New Yorker.

My father was lying on the futon in the front room, watching us and talking to Gordon. Gordon was animated with nervous energy and he talked about the evils of Catholicism and life on the streets;

strange things that he shared in great detail with me, an eleven-year-old kid from the rural North. He slept the entire day and emerged at night, so I usually got to talk to him before I went to bed. Whatever Gordon's business, it required him to leave the apartment late at night to make his rounds.

I remember him telling my father about a fight he had with a famous writer. Apparently the fight was over a woman. Words were exchanged when they passed each other on the street and then they started brawling and eventually ended up wrestling on the ground. Much to each man's surprise and embarrassment, Gordon's thumb ended up in the writer's ass and quickly ended the fight. That is what I was told. Gordon's life was dangerous. My father tells me he was recently robbed and seriously beaten. He did not report the incident to the police, though. For some people, there is no shelter.

The holiday celebration at Bobby's apartment had reached its height, and it was in the midst of that sensorial deluge that Dido enticed my brother and me to smoke. We were now pitching quarters and the snow had stopped falling. The radiator shook as the steam was forced through it. In the commotion of music and wine pouring into glasses and condensed breath dripping from the windows, Dido announced that he was going to leave a joint on the window sill and if anything happened to it, well, he didn't know anything about it. My brother quickly responded to Dido's invitation and slid the joint behind his ear, where it disappeared beneath his long, wavy brown hair.

Not long after that, Dido suggested the two of us head to the rooftop to see the "Q" (short for "Montague Street") strung with Christmas lights. "Where are you two going?" my father asked as my brother carefully removed the security bar from the door. My father wore jeans, a white oxford, and wool socks, which he rubbed together in a self-perpetuating cycle of itching and scratching and static discharge. I knew we were up to no good and I could not get my tongue to work. My brother knew to answer the question and only the question, which is exactly what he did. Then we slipped out into the hall and closed the door behind us. My brother and I could hear people living their lives behind the doors: They did dishes and listened to music and talked on the telephone. Everyday things that seemed strange when done out of sight.

The roof was unlit and covered in a light snow. We walked to the edge and the wind there moved heavily and pushed at us like a demon in a dream. At that hour few people were about, but the come-and-gone had left their tracks in the snow and they trailed off down toward East River, which from this distance flowed noiseless and unseen. As promised, the "Q" was lit with thousands of lights that reflected off the snow and off the butcher's glass and meats ensconced in tinsel across the street. I turned to ask my brother if that was a pig's head with a very red apple in its mouth, but he had already stepped back out of the wind and was attempting to light the joint. After his third attempt the tip of joint burned like a small hot eye, and it burned brighter still and bathed his mouth in a warm glow as he drew from it. He cupped it like a pro and handed it to me.

I didn't need any help because, like every other normal child, I was hard-wired for sucking. Having experimented with cigarettes, and since I had asthma, I was a little fearful of the smoke, which I was sure would burn my lungs and send me into a fit of coughing. So like Bill Clinton, I didn't inhale. Instead I held it in my mouth and tasted it: a mixture of rich soil, dark chocolate, and a hint of perfume. When my brother took back the joint and inhaled, the light from the cherry lit my face and he could see that my cheeks were inflated like the nut-packed cheeks of a squirrel. He left the joint in his mouth and popped my cheeks with his index fingers. A pale cloud of smoke burst from my mouth.

"Just take a small hit and hold it," he said as he gave me the joint.

"Okay," I said.

The joint was just over an inch long by now and the smoke was very hot and tasty in an unexpected way. As if it were a spoonful of hot soup, I let it sit there and cool for a few seconds. Then I inhaled. I watched Christian for the sign that it was time to exhale. He stubbed out the roach and slipped it inside a matchbook for safekeeping. "Okay, let it out." I exhaled until I was sure my lungs were flat as paper sacks.

As we descended from the roof, my brother reminded me not to act goofy or suspicious. I considered his request and was sure I didn't know how I was going to avoid either behavior since they came so naturally anyway.

"Don't worry, I won't," I said.

"So what are you going to do?" he asked quickly.

"I don't know. Eat some pie or something. Mind my business." We were both standing at the door to Bobby's apartment and Christian had his hand on the knob.

"That is the worst thing you could do. Give it a few minutes before you start eating, okay?"

I stood there, transfixed. "Okay," I replied. "Are you going to turn the knob?"

I used Christian as a kind of shield as we walked inside. It would have been obvious had any one thought to notice, but the once festive apartment was now quiet. My father was still on the futon and he put down the book he was reading and pulled off his glasses and laid them on the book. "How was it up there?" My brother and I stopped mid-stride, but thankfully Christian took the initiative and addressed the question, which from my perspective was simply too complicated to answer. Besides, I felt like a great vat of new feelings and nerve endings; like a moon jellyfish undulating and gathering information and nutrients from the deep ocean. I was embodied energy and I was sure I had all this power to change the world, but all I could think to do was sit at the little kitchen table and ask for some pie.

Bobby was doing the dishes in a short red satin robe with a floral print. I think he had just returned from Florida because he was very tan. "Hey, there's little Max," Bobby said excitedly as I pulled out a chair and sat at the table. He tumbled a glass in a soft white towel and inspected it as he did so. When it was spotless, he smiled and placed it on the shelf, put down the towel, and plunged his hands into the warm, soapy water, where he searched for silverware.

"Can I get you anything?" he asked.

I glanced in the other room where my father and brother were talking about something on the television.

"May I have some pie, please?"

My brother apparently had his radar adjusted for the word *pie* because at the exact moment I spoke it he shot me a hot look that said, *I told you to wait a few minutes before asking for pie!* My shoulders sunk and I lowered my head and mouthed the words, *But I'm hungry.*

"Of course you may have some pie," Bobby said. "Will Big Max mind?" Bobby's eyebrows lifted, but he had no intention of asking my father if I could have pie. He was just going through the motions and doing what he thought he should as someone who had my best interest in mind. I'm not sure, but I think we were poor and didn't get to eat sugar very much. Rather than withholding good things, Bobby would lavish them upon me. Dollar bills and sweets.

"No, I don't think he would mind," I said, ruefully.

"Good. Then I shall cut you a big wedge of pie."

As Bobby turned on the oven to warm the pie, he would alter-
nate humming and singing a song from back in the day. Trouble is, his
voice was high and nasal and, when attempting to hit certain notes,
reminded me of Kathryn Hepburn's faltering voice. I could handle
Bobby's singing and appearance separately, but together they were too
much, and I started giggling, softly, at first. Then I saw my brother
looking at me with that look he gets when he's trying not to laugh or is
about to say something funny and his mouth tilts sideways and purses.
That was all it took to send me into a fit of laughter. Bobby looked
over at me briefly, but he didn't seem fazed by my outburst. I held my
stomach, doubled over, and watched laughing tears drip on the table.
I looked behind me and saw that my brother was upside down. I tried
to figure out why he wasn't laughing and that is when I saw my father
peeking around the corner.

He was concerned, not for me, but for Bobby, who he rightly
guessed was the subject of my laughing fit. Then my father looked at
Bobby and suddenly the look of concern softened a little. Whether
or not my father understood why I was laughing, I didn't want to
hurt Bobby's feelings. Nor did I want to anger my father. I recalled
his ire one evening when he, Christian, and I were eating at Yusef's,
which in those days was one of two fancy restaurants in Caribou. My
brother had ordered the sweet-and-sour pork for its sweetness and
had decided he was going to use a knife instead of a fork to convey his
food. My father asked him to do otherwise, but Christian is stubborn
and continued to use his knife. As my brother stabbed his third piece
of pork, my father threw a glass of water on him.

I interpreted my father's expression through that filter. A few seconds later I got ahold of myself. Then Bobby started singing again and that sent me into another fit. Rather than fight it, I got up and jumped on the futon with my brother and father. "What's so funny?" my father asked as he rubbed my head and the three of us snuggled. "Why are you boys laughing?" Then he started laughing himself and the three of us became a giggling heap of legs, heads, and arms. We must have been quite a sight. And thus it was in the company of two people I loved most in the world that I first gave myself to the laughter and euphoria of the drug.

I could hear Bobby open the stove and remove the pie. Then he leaned in the doorway with the dish towel over his shoulder and his legs slightly crossed at the knee. He smiled like a flamboyant and benevolent grandmother. As the pie cooled on the table, the snow started falling again. I remember watching the large white flakes pile on the black steel of the fire escape. Later I slept and dreamed it fell until the river and the valleys of the city were filled and the lights of the tallest buildings shined under the snow like death beds for lost birds and childhood dreamers. Now my dreams safely destroy what otherwise might be real.

★ ★ ★

Last night I dreamed that Kim left me. We were living in Spain and from outside the dream I was pleased we had finally made good on our threats to leave the United States, which had gone insane with religiosity, materialism, and greed. We had stayed out late, eating chocolate and drinking cold beer. We watched the fog roll up from the sea and saw how it filled the small valley and hid the goats as they sought a place to sleep under the almond trees.

We measured the chill with our bones, which we warmed at a fire by whose light I saw that her lips were damp with muscatel and the spittle of profanities she used to describe her love for me. In the dream I said I was going to leave if she did not comply with some wish of mine. *Don't bother*, she said, and then she disappeared from my life. *Poof.* Her disappearance was impossibly sudden. The medium of the dream is very efficient.

Thus all the consequences of our separation assailed me at once. When I realized my children were gone, too, I was overcome by emptiness and sadness. I often wonder how my own father survived our absence when we finally boarded the plane for Salt Lake. What point must one come to in order to accept such profound loss? Once destruction is set in motion, it can be slowed but not stopped except through collision with something of equal force. In my dream it was as if Kim, Wilder, and Greer had simply stepped off the face of the Earth. I had just started living into this awful feeling when I was awakened by Wilder who, from his own dream, called out "Daddy" and then fell back to sleep.

★ ★ ★

I feel like I've spent years waiting for a moon that never rises.

★ ★ ★

I would never blame my parents for the life we had growing up: they did what they could. My father and mother stayed in a loveless marriage for as long as they could. When I think of living a single day in conflict with Kim, I don't know how either of them lasted ten years. And yet I doubt they were thinking about how children who grow up in single-parent households may be more likely to find trouble and to keep it once it is found. Unlike Kim, for whom trouble came largely in the form of staying out past dark and talking back to her parents, I was drawn to chemicals, including marijuana (the most innocuous outlet), alcohol (by far the most destructive), cocaine (known by users as the "evil drug"), magic mushrooms, and LSD.

Although I had friends who used hallucinogens or "tripped" in excess (the usual dose of acid was a single "hit," but I had friends who would drop ten, twenty hits at one time), I can count on three hands the number of times I took acid. I don't know exactly how many times I did mushrooms, but it was under ten. Drugs and alcohol were omnipresent when I was growing up, as I am sure they are now. I can only speculate about why sobriety was out of the question for so many of the kids I knew growing up.

Most of the people I knew were middle class and had plenty of choices, yet the majority chose some form of inebriation. We had not learned to appreciate the joy that comes with being alive. Over coffee, Utah peaches, and toast, I shared these insights with Kim. "Who knows how things may have been different had I not partaken?" I mused, wistfully. Kim wiped a blob of yogurt from Greer's face. Then she raised her eyebrows and nodded. Feeling emboldened by her show of sympathy, I said, "Maybe I could have been president."

One has almost got to become a connoisseur of natural "highs" because they are so subtle and short-lived compared to their synthetic counterparts. As an early teenager, I didn't have the discipline or desire to create or wait for natural highs, which could not compete with smoking a joint, drinking a six-pack, gobbling mushrooms, or dropping a hit of acid. I have since learned to notice the intensity of even the smallest natural pleasure. Peaches again come to mind, as does the cool air of morning or night, the smell of rain, and watching Wilder and Greer pick raspberries in our backyard. This change in perspective makes perfect sense, if only because the cares of a fifteen-year-old boy are not the concerns of a forty-year-old man, whose awareness of time passing pressurizes life and clarifies its brevity and sweetness. I am aware of the need to self-preserve.

Whether I make decisions for my sake or for the sake of my children, all my reasons are selfish. I can't breathe without being selfish. Sometimes the people in my life benefit from what I do. I wish the planet did, too, but I'm afraid it doesn't, which, when I think about it, fills me with worry. Over the last few years I have gotten better at controlling my worry and calculating my choices. But even as a young man I had a keen sense of my limitations. This was especially true with drugs, which I both craved and feared. With one or two exceptions, I did drugs only in the wilderness, usually at Bell Canyon Reservoir.

In dark or moonlit woods, I did not worry about uncontrollable social encounters. Now that the predators are mostly dead, the natural environment is relatively safe compared to an urban environment. Nature also helped to preserve the drug's function as a temporary reprieve from monotony. The kids who could not adhere to this simple rule invariably developed the greatest problems with drugs. I've had close calls, but luckily I avoided forming long-term relationships with everything except cigarettes.

My hope is that my own children will not take the chances I did growing up, which is mildly hypocritical since it is mostly with pleasure that I recall my youthful indiscretions. My history of drug use is also a history of people and places, many of which are gone or have changed to the point where they may as well be. But some of the places have persisted, and as long as they exist, maybe I still have a chance to understand the past. We are fleshed with place. Our words leave us and flutter in the brain's nebula, and when no one is there to hear them they drift unmoored through the unyielding expanse we call time and space.

★ ★ ★

When my father, brother, and I last visited Bell Canyon Reservoir, which was by far my most treasured haunt, I stood for a very long time on a certain familiar rock overlooking the water. I had stood there some twenty years before in the dead of the night, leaning into the desert wind, smelling the sage and the water and the cooling, sun-warmed granite, watching a million moons blinking on the wind-torn surface of the water, which in that year had risen so high it was flush with the road and I could have taken one effortless step into it.

A group of about ten of us had dropped acid and felt like getting close to the moon. We had a couple hours before it would appear above Lone Peak and so we spiraled around the reservoir and into trees, where, without light, we hoped to make a fire. Where we walked a seep had saturated the ground and I remember the hollow, sucking sounds of the mud that eventually tore off my friend Tully's shoe.

The other girls laughed and plopped down in dark, wet richness and then clawed at the mud to find Tully's shoe. They sat with their legs apart and I saw flashes of supple inner thighs and an undone silver pant button. Teeth flashing. Later we found a grassy area where deer had bedded down. A couple of the boys began the search for wood. I sat in the grass and noticed a resounding hum that emanated from the rocks and trees and starlight.

Finally someone lit the fire and I don't think we spoke a word while it burned. No one fed it and soon it turned to hot coals and then to dead ash and we got up and walked through the damp snake grass back to the reservoir. I found myself far ahead of the group and standing on that rock above the water.

I soon realized Tully was standing beside me with her eyes closed against the desert grit and she had the seeds of a smile on her face. Her hair was thick and black and, were it not for the moon, it would have disappeared against the backdrop of night. I remember trying to think of words to say to her, to make something of the night and of our standing there, but everything was so obvious: the water and the moon and us standing there, alone. Maybe I should have asked her to open her eyes and look at me. I don't know. How is it that even then this part of my life felt too late? On that night over twenty years ago, there was nothing to be done except stand there pulsing in the darkness, casting furtive glances at Tully's complicated beauty.

I doubt whether "complicated" fully explains what I mean, though, so when Kim comes into the dining room where I am writing I ask if there is a better way to describe her. Until now Wilder has been focusing on typing his name on an old laptop, but the moment he hears me talking about girls (or "girdles," as he calls them), he starts asking questions. First he wants to know why I "like that girdle." Were Tully alive it would be a simple enough question, but she's not and for some reason the question throws me off balance. I suppose all I had to do was reformulate it using the past tense, as in *Why did I like Tully?* or *I liked Tully because* . . . But I felt obligated to answer the question as it stood. "Well, let me see. I'm not really sure, Wilder. That's a tricky question."

Wilder furrows his brow and tilts his head and flexes the muscles on either side of his nose. He looks funny and I feel the room in me that holds laughter start to open. Through the crack in the door I can see my four-year-old self peeking out, and behind me are all the friends I've ever had, including the dogs and the cats. As much as I want to laugh, I can't escape the gravity of the question. Luckily, when Kim sees me struggling she explains to Wilder that Daddy and Uncle Christian were friends with Tully and that I was writing about her in my book. Of course nothing is very simple: Way leads on to way and he wants to know why.

Kim and I look at each other. Again I don't have an answer, but Kim says "Daddy is writing about her because he was friends with her and her life was tragic." Kim knows Wilder will not understand what she means by *tragic*, so she quickly adds that Tully experienced a lot of sad things over the course of her short life. That does the trick as far as Wilder is concerned. The more I think about it, however, the more disconcerted I become.

Tully's beauty was complicated because it was wild and broken and is still hard to let go of precisely for that reason. She had night-black eyes, full red lips and, during the last years of her life, a pale face. This was not because she was wary of the sun: On a drive up the canyon, she had been looking out the window watching the autumn leaves when she was in a head-on car accident. Having shattered her face on the windshield, she had a twelve-inch, pink and tender-looking scar that ran from her brow, past the corner of her left eye, and across her cheek.

The glass had sliced her tear duct and so her eye was always watering, unless she dabbed it with a handkerchief or the sleeve of her shirt. Usually she just let it water. This accident may have killed something inside of her, but it did not kill all of her. She wouldn't be so fortunate a few years later out near Horse Lake, where she was thrown from the back of a motorcycle. What if that deer had not leapt out, causing the driver to swerve and jettison Tully into the hard mountain dark? Would she still be wild at forty, driving the sidewalks of Salt Lake with a mixed drink between her legs and a brain numbed by cocaine?

*We shoot off the sidewalk and back into the street. Newspapers flap
their wings. I've got both hands on the dashboard.*

*"Where do you want to go?" she asks, with a sly smile. Her mouth is
bursting with ice and lime.*

"But where can we?" I reply.

Dying is a natural process, like closing up a beach house in winter.
When the wind gets in there, the doors to the rooms may close all at
once if we're lucky. I wonder if my dead friends are sitting inside those
rooms with the doors open, waiting for me to shuffle down the long
hall with a candle and close them.

I would dream about Tully for years after her death. In one dream
I was lying face up in a field. I was happy to look at the stars, feel the
cool earth on my back and, finally, to know how stones must feel.
Then someone touches my face. I turn and see Tully lying there beside
me. She smiles at me reassuringly, and in the calm black pools of her
eyes, I see that I am bones.

My brother Christian was no longer dating Tully at the time of her
death, but they had gone together for a couple years, and so under-
standably he took her death very personally. I wouldn't realize how
personally until eight years later, when I would come across a video
montage he had made to memorialize her passing. The montage
consists of black-and-white stills shot inside a burned-down school.
Despite its technological limitations, the piece is fluid and disturbing.

Although I wouldn't actually find the montage until several years
after he had made it, I remember stopping by his apartment one night
in November of 1993 and finding him working on it. I'm sure of this
date because I was preparing to go to Spain with my father the following January and I needed a photograph to submit with my pass-
port application. It had been a little over a year since Tully died, but

Christian didn't once use her name in my presence and I didn't think to ask what had inspired the montage.

"Do you want to talk to Steve?" Christian asked. "Steve" was code for marijuana. "Gary" was code for mushrooms. I don't recall whether acid and cocaine ever got their own names. If I were to name them now, they would be *Space Hatch* and *Zombie Dust*. Steve's name got used a lot. I see myself on the phone on a Friday night: "Did you talk to Steve?" or "Whose party? Is Steve going to be there?" And so on. I'm surprised my mother never asked, "Who is Steve? One of your friends from school?" Well, she had her hands full working a job and raising three teenagers alone.

"I haven't talked to Steve in a while," I replied as I took the joint and took a small hit. Apart from being a self-described lightweight, I had learned to be cautious when smoking grass. It takes only one experience—bad or good—to change the direction of one's life or, in this case, attitude toward ganja. Mine came in the ninth grade, when my friend Billy Rat and I had smoked some weed that I later discovered was laced with PCP. We smoked out behind the gym at school with this other kid I didn't know or like and then went back to class. I sat in the back and dry-heaved with my head on the desk.

I looked up once at Billy Rat who sat four desks up, and I saw him looking back at me, as if to ask, "Do you feel sick as fuck, too?" One look at me and I'm sure he got his answer, as did I: pale-green face, dark beds beneath his wrecked eyes. He looked like I felt, but he also had this shit-eating grin on his face that made me laugh hard and offered a short reprieve from my stomach's revolution. Despite looking at me with concern, not one of my teachers asked me if I were alright. Three hours later, I called my mom and told her I needed to come home. I was sick for a week. My mother had no clue.

"Want to use some Visine?" Christian asked from behind the camera. "Your eyes look a little fiery." I went into the bathroom to get the Visine and instead cupped some cold water to my eyes and then tamped them dry. Behind me I could see the radiator behind which our friend Ticky had stuffed his soiled underwear. Christian had discovered them there and puzzled over whose they were until he recalled the last time he had seen Ticky. He had dropped by one evening with a quarter gram of coke. Ticky had started with an 8-Ball, which is a gram, and he had been snorting all night. Christian had planned to spend the evening with a girl he had met when Ticky showed up uninvited.

If Ticky were in his right mind and not Ticky, he would have looked inside, seen that Christian was with a girl, and been on his way. But Ticky was an invader with the smooth, bright face of a twelve-year-old. My brother's good manners, empathy, and mild passivity could not compete with Ticky's man-child cocktail of alcohol, cocaine, and surging testosterone. If his testosterone explained his success with young women (as well as his willingness to insert himself between my brother and his amorous pursuit), it may have also been the cause of his early hair loss.

Although Ticky had lost all the hair atop his head, he could still grow what resembled an airy blond hula skirt of hair, which he complemented with a bandanna. Together, his hair, face, and the bandanna made for an interesting interpretive event. Still, there was no denying Ticky's ability to woo the women right out from under a mild-mannered young man like my brother.

Christian was therefore relieved when Ticky disappeared into the bathroom about an hour after arriving. He was in there for about an hour, which is a really long time for a guy in his early twenties. Christian would later deduce that the coke was laced with laxative and that Ticky had shit himself or sharted and then hid the evidence behind the radiator. "What the hell was he thinking?" Christian would later muse. One can really tell a lot about someone's frame of mind by how he hides his shitty underwear. "Did he think I wouldn't find them?" Ticky may have been counting on the fact that Christian couldn't smell due to a head injury he had gotten in a skateboarding accident. When I suggested this possibility to Christian, he shook his head and could only speculate about how many friends had used the bathroom, seen the underwear, and attributed Ticky's calling card to him.

The cold water had done its job and shrunk the slight puffiness beneath my eyes. I walked back into the living room where all the camera equipment was set up. I readied myself for the photograph. "On the count of three, look straight into the camera and give me 'the look.'" After the photograph had been taken, I hung out while Christian worked on the montage. He looked at me and put his finger to his lips. Then he turned on a somber instrumental piece and the video recorder. As the two played, Christian would blow cigarette smoke into the frames so that they appeared ghostly and smoldering. Although juvenile, many years later when I would finally view the complete montage, the piece undid me. If I were a pile of balancing stones, this record of my brother's pain was the tremor that sent me crashing.

I was living in Arizona and had been home alone for days. This was long before the birth of our children, and Kim was in Mississippi visiting her parents. I was smoking from a bag of cheap dope my brother had given me a year before when I was visiting Salt Lake. I had also chugged a couple of beers and I thought I was happy. But then I turned on the video machine and a black-and-white still of Tully in fishnet stockings and a satin top flashed across the screen. Then another image appeared, this time of her lying on a couch with her thick black hair spilling over the armrest. An Italian Marilyn Monroe, her right arm is down beside her so that the back of her wrist touches the floor. I sat there and watched the whole thing. Then I cracked another beer and cried.

I've always loved my brother, but he is not easy to know. As we've gotten older, it is not that we have gotten to know each other better, necessarily. It is that I accept that I may never know him beyond this point. I knew him well enough to call him that night and tell him about the video I had found. I cried and cried because, as I told him, I felt ashamed that I had not realized how much Tully had meant to him. "It's alright," he kept saying. "It's not a big deal." I was twenty-three when Tully died. I was just about to graduate from the University of Utah and was preparing applications for graduate school. I was moving on and I was self-absorbed. I felt terrible about Tully, but I didn't dwell on her unless she invaded my dreams.

After the initial sadness, Christian didn't say that he was having a hard time dealing with Tully's death. And they hadn't dated for years. Like every other teen couple, they had their share of fights. Although the fights would become more violent, in the early years of their relationship, back when he was about eighteen and she was about seventeen, they would fight about sex or, as it happened, about not having it. My sister Nicole was living with my grandmother in Idaho, but Christian and I still lived at home with my mother in Sandy. I was on my way somewhere when I overheard Christian arguing on the telephone. "Look, if I don't want to, I don't want to. Sometimes I just don't feel like it." Then Tully said something and Christian said, "Why is that so hard for you to understand?"

This went for a few minutes and then Christian hung up the phone. "Fuck me," he said emphatically.

I remember standing in the doorway and smiling ear to ear. "Why aren't you putting out, man?" I laughed. Christian smiled his funny little smile. "She's driving me crazy." I stepped back inside and closed the door. "I can't believe what I just heard," I said. Christian looked at me and shrugged his shoulders. I could see that he didn't want to discuss it, so I said, "I wish I had your problem," and left it at that.

How the days change is strange and stranger still is that I get to watch and feel them unravel around me like tongues of smoke. A few years ago and several years after she had died, I passed Tully on the road for the last time. My brother was sitting next to her with his arm out the window. He saw me and said something to Tully. I heard music as they passed. I pulled the car off the road and watched them in the rearview mirror. I thought Tully was going to turn the car around so my brother and I could talk. But she didn't. She kept on driving.

★ ★ ★

Other than their bodies, most teenagers don't have much going for them. Of course there were some exceptions and I knew a few of them, but generally the emphasis was on how to make the body feel good. I suppose if I had lived in a more progressive state, I might have had more opportunities to realize my hedonism. Then, as now, the dominant culture of Mormonism was heavily concentrated in rural and suburban areas, including Sandy, which is where I lived for many years before finally getting an apartment in the liberal stronghold of downtown Salt Lake. The prevailing religion was like a damp and suffocating blanket beneath which I could disappear and, if I did not occasionally come up for air, slowly die. In the pious environment of suburban Utah, there were too few of us to disrupt the mainstream and the little would-be theocrats who, even with their tentative hold on religious tenets, ruled the microcosm by virtue of their numbers.

I had no incentive to regularly interact with Mormon boys, but I dated a few Mormon girls and except for their tails snipped at birth and their sawed-off horns, they were basically indistinguishable from their nonreligious counterparts. They seemed to enjoy their bodies, which they treated like secrets or dark chocolates children hide under their beds and enjoy when everyone was asleep, but at the end of the night, their need to be "good" girls was usually stronger than their corporeal cravings and curiosity. This conflict between the secular and the sacred no doubt explains why every religious girl I knew had perfected the rough art of dry humping, an activity that apparently allowed the girls to express desire without desecrating the temple. The problem, however, is that the more beautiful the edifice, the stronger is the desire to lie with the god inside it.

Mormons are notorious for what, from the outside, appear to be hasty marriages. My mother's sister has ten grown children, and I don't think a single one of them knew her husband or his wife for more than a few months before marrying. The truth is, Mormon boys are like other boys. They have penises with which they attempt to realize their needs and fulfill their desires. But the rules are the rules: no coitus before marriage. So is it a wonder that, in record time, Mormon boys marry the first pretty thing that comes along?

I know there is more to it. There always is. For instance, Mormon girls are among the most beautiful on the planet. And yet as a sixteen-year-old outsider, who could not fathom converting or marrying, usually I could not bring myself to expend energy for nominal benefits, including the friction from so-and-so's cutoff Levis. During my last year of high school, I would meet, date, and then lose a beautiful Mormon girl named Dee, who, in addition to being the only exception to this rule, was also a painful illustration of it that haunts me to this day. Fortunately there was no shortage of non-Mormon girls on whom I could lavish my affections.

I am reluctant to revisit those early relationships if only because they contrast so sharply with my present relationship with Kim, my partner of over twenty years, best friend, and the mother of my children. To compare the love between a couple of teenagers and the bond between the same couple thirty years later is to find that love is like everything else: over time, its meanings slough and change and become unrecognizable. And sometimes it dies a death that is no more preventable than our own. In terms of corporeal excitement, what stage of the relationship can compare with the initial stages of courtship and just after? Having lived in the throes of such chemical heat, unwise lovers long to return to an earlier time once the courtship stage has passed. Most of my early relationships did not last beyond these early stages. In spite of how well our bodies appealed to each other, we weren't equipped to love beyond them.

To the extent that most of my relationships were short-lived and intense, they were like drugs. How else to explain the wonderful and reckless things I did in those days? After being caught drinking thanks to Brody's reckless driving in the high school parking lot, I was kicked out of public school for the last time and henceforth attended Valley High, which was an alternative school for kids who otherwise might have dropped out altogether. While there I met a young girl who I will call Lark Rodriguez. She was like that one palm-size, smooth dark stone found in a riverbed of white granite. Perhaps this is why I

remember so well the first time I saw her walking down the main hall
of the old school building. It was evening and the hall was lit by orange
lights and she smiled at me warmly. Valley was such a small school and
so few people attended that it was strange and magical when this dark
flower appeared.

I remember her body. We had driven into the foothills above the
state capitol where the city lights spread out before us like a million
just fallen stars, smoldering white-hot out there in the welling darkness. We circled around the horseshoe-shaped road that skirts City
Creek Canyon and I tried to find the precise spot on Gravity Hill,
where by law the car should have rolled backward but instead rolled
forward up the hill and thus seemed to defy gravity. In the fall air the
heavy odor of decomposing leaves and wet sage came on a wind from
higher up the mountain. The deer were on the move and now and
then I could see them silhouetted against the graying sky. There was
no moon and so it was one less thing to talk about. The road was black
except for where the beams of my headlights cut a forty-foot swathe
into the future night.

I couldn't find the place where I could take the car out of gear and
then roll up the hill, so I slowed and looked at the smooth white hills
beneath Lark's sweater and then at her eyes. When I saw that she had
been looking at me, I looked down at her smiling mouth. We drove
through the empty streets of a Sunday night in Salt Lake, talking
about I can't imagine what, and I saw the road with one eye and with
the other I watched Lark's thighs close and spread with the movement
of the car. Sometimes I could see her profile, but most of the time she
fixed me with her eyes and I felt the fist of blood pounding in my chest
like a great drum announcing the oldest knowledge, a preamble to the
grinding nuclei dividing in the spume.

I pulled off the road somewhere along Gravity Hill and we walked into the big, warm wind that had come off the lake smelling of brine and dust and the first whiff of sulfurous cold of the storm that was building somewhere far out in the west desert. Lark wore a long, black coat and gloves to match and I thought that at any moment she was going to lift up into the night like some great woolen bird and take me with her. Then the wind would double back and I would smell the faint perfume of her hair, which lashed wildly.

Earlier in the evening she had lectured me on the strife of her amorous history, and though she did not provide details, I knew she considered herself wounded and that I had been warned. But a wounded god is still a god; I would take what I could get. We had walked maybe a hundred yards when the first large, white flakes of snow started falling.

"Should we turn back?" she asked, looking into the sky.

"I think so," I said, both anxious and afraid of whatever conclusion the night might bring.

When we got back to the car, we brushed off the snow and sat, our faces flushed with cold and steaming. Lark had turned in her seat so that her back was against the door.

"What should we do now?" I asked. Her coat was open and I could see the snow melting on her neck.

"Maybe you should just take me home."

"Okay," I said, as if the night were of no consequence.

We did not speak as I drove the few miles to her house and pulled into the driveway. "Wait here." Lark got out of the car and on the wind came her candied fragrance and the cold leafy smell of late October. Then she disappeared into the house. A few minutes later she reappeared.

"Want to come in?" she asked, leaning in through the open passenger door.

"Will your parents mind?"

"They're upstairs in their room watching TV," she smiled. "They won't bother us."

Lark closed the door and waited for me outside with her arms folded high on her chest. I thought of a crow wrapping itself in its wings. I turned off the car and we went inside. Lark's hand was small, soft, and cold and with it she led me quickly past the hall leading to her parents' room. Apart from the light from their room and the sound of their muted voices coming from their open door, her parents did not appear. They were ideas, vaguely defined, apparitional, but enough to inspire vigilance.

The TV was on and the couch was warm from where Lark's parents had been sitting before Lark had driven them upstairs. We hadn't been there for five minutes when Lark placed her hand in the valley between my crotch and thigh. I could feel the heat from her hand as it became more certain, sinking, rising and sinking again until finally she found the periphery of my special purpose, my package, my gift to whoever would take it. My body pulsed as if my heart were beating between my legs and I could not devise one complex thought if my life depended on it. Lark's eyes were soft with desire. We listened to her parents moving around and talking upstairs. "I know what we can do," she whispered. Her breath was warm and smelled like winter candy. A hot madness swept over me. *Is this what Huey Lewis meant when he sang of a new drug?* I wondered.

Somewhere in the failing light of the dry season a goat was bleeding out from a cut in its throat and ten million birds rose from a dead sea and tumbled like a wave across the dust-stained sun. I became a body, simplified and driven by the oldest brain. I was expecting her to lead me to a secret chamber, perhaps one entered through a door hidden behind a painting or a piece of furniture, but Lark rose and took me by both hands to lead me behind the couch, where she lay on the floor and invited me down. I was careful not to lay all my weight atop her and thus undermine access to her body.

I could feel her heat. Lark reached for my pant buttons and I waved her off. "Wait," I whispered and without opening her eyes she slid her hands down to the small of my back. I could not take my eyes off of her as she writhed beneath me. I was pleased by my apparent effectiveness, but soon I realized that all I had done was set this event in motion, as if at any moment I could leave and she would go on without me. She was abandoned to trance or to waking sleep or to voodoo dream.

Lark's mother called to her from atop the stairs and reminded her to let in the cat. We both froze and listened. I could see the sliding glass door and a large orange cat sitting outside it, watching me. It looked perturbed and accusatory. By then I had Lark's pants pulled down below her knees and I had pushed her sweater up to the base of her neck and unclasped her bra.

"Okay," Lark called to her mother, propped up on her elbows. We listened for a moment more.

"Should we stop?" I asked.

"Do you want to?"

"If you do."

"I don't if you don't."

"I don't," I said, drifting down her body, kissing her lowest rib, stomach, and the high dunes of her pelvis.

Eventually my head was between her thighs and my hands were on her breasts, and then without any training or experience, I proceeded.

I could taste faint salt and the melon fragrance of soap. Lark had her hands in my hair and gushed a silken guava. Things were going well. Until I realized that the tip of my organ had come out of my pants and that I was mindlessly rubbing it raw in the carpet. *For Christ's sake,* I whispered, and then I slid up and kissed Lark deeply and this time I did not stop her when she unbuttoned my pants and had at me, first with her hand and then with her mouth. When that didn't work she pulled me inside. I glanced at the screen door and saw the cat huddled against the window with its eyes closed. A light snow had collected on its head and back.

Normally I could not afford to lose concentration, but I had been holding my piss for the last half-hour and my spigot had set up like a rill of concrete. Urine: It's the poor man's Viagra. When Lark came her entire body tensed and she arched backward like a dark flower in the wind and drew herself up so that her stomach pressed against mine and her hair skimmed the floor. As if chilled she shuddered a little. Seeing I was still hard, Lark asked if there were anything she could do. I said, "No, that's okay, I've got to go," and I carefully bent the tree back into my pants and added that I had to get my mother's car home.

I might have been lying, but I followed with a promise I would call her that night. I kept my word and after some small talk she described her ideal love as if she both did and did not have me in mind.

"And what about sex?" I asked her, certain that I had rewritten the book thanks to a full bladder. She became very thoughtful, which she signaled by pausing and making musing sounds.

"I think if spirits could fuck, that is how it should feel."

I had never really thought much about hell until I met Lark. The night she lectured me about her past she also announced her commitment to God as a good Catholic and how she would like it very much if her lover were to feel the same way. But then the night at her house happened and I couldn't figure out what part of her was supposed to be Catholic.

I remember seeing a low-budget movie about a handsome young priest who, despite his vows to God, struggled with corporeal desire, the meat puppet in his pants. Sensing this, and knowing better than anyone else a man's sexual appetite, the devil morphed into a scantily clad, buxom beauty and attempted to seduce the priest and capture his soul. Were the priest a sixteen-year-old boy, it would be a done deal. In fact, if teenage boys could sell their souls for a night with a beautiful woman, satellite imagery would reveal a human chain of them, winding round and round the world: One by one, the boys would step up and ask *Where do I sign?* But the priest is chaste, so it takes him about ten minutes to give it up. I sat there thinking, *Hurry, before she disappears into the fiery well* (which symbolically and for convenience is located in the church's basement). Beneath my cavalier attitude, however, I was mindful of hell and of the fact that this busty beauty was really a man who smelled like fire and would lay waste to my needful flesh. For religious people, many of whom I knew growing up and who still surround me even now, sex is of the body and the body is of death; hell is home to blood mites and to the eyeless white worms that hunt them and mate in the rancid chinks of the somatic dark.

★ ★ ★

My mother told me that if I wanted to avoid foul dreams and a sour morning, I should not do certain things before bed. The list of what not to do is a matter of personal preference. One person might avoid fighting with a spouse, whereas another person won't watch scary movies or look at dirty magazines for fear of fucking up a wet dream.

To my own list of things not to do before bed, which includes drinking a lot of water and eating a big meal, I would have to add deciding to put down my thirteen-year-old cat the next day. This last item has a corollary, which is how, in addition to dealing with my own feelings of loss, I am going to explain to my children the cat's sudden and perpetual absence even as I hope they don't realize that if the cat can disappear without notice, so can Kim and I.

These questions and questions like them have the effect of keeping me up at night. Do not pose them. Put them off until morning. They won't be any easier to answer, but at least you will have gotten a full night's sleep, which means you'll have a clear head to better concoct the long-lived and intricate lie you will tell your own children.

Don't think that because you are talking to children the lie won't need to be complex. It will have several moving parts, and if you're not careful, you might get caught in it, which would be your own fault because you warned your children to be mindful around people and machines.

★ ★ ★

My friend Cleese had run away from home and was living in an old silver mine not far from Bell Canyon Reservoir and the mouth of Little Cottonwood Canyon. My friend Dilson and I brought him supplies several times over the course of his stay. Mostly canned food, water, and cigarettes. A raft of us—including me, Christian, Dilson, and Dilson's older brother, Curtis—worked at The Peacock, an upscale restaurant near the mouth, and one night after I finished my shift I was supposed to pick up Dilson and drive up to the mine. I didn't really care for mines, but I was pretty sure Dilson had some nose candy he was aching to snort and I wanted to help him.

When I walked outside, he was already there, waiting behind my car, smoking a cigarette.

"What are you doing here, man?" I asked.

Dilson flicked his cigarette into a puddle. He turned just so and his glasses and helmet of hair caught the light.

"I got antsy. Is Rusty working?" Beneath his cap of short, tight-blonde curls, Dilson's jaw sawed back and forth and his tongue sounded sticky. He had camel jaw, which meant he had been sampling.

"Yeah, he is," I said. "He's about to get off." Dilson lit another cigarette and walked around to the passenger side of my car.

"Let's get the fuck out of here then."

Rusty dealt coke and the night before someone had stolen a baggy from his coat pocket. When he came charging out of the pantry swearing and promising death to whoever it was that had stolen from him, I knew instantly that it was Dilson. He had gotten off work not five minutes before and as he was leaving I asked, *Where you going, Dilweed?* and he looked back at me with this crazed look and I thought, *Jesus Christ, who did you kill?*

I was working behind the counter with my brother and Curtis as Rusty stormed the kitchen, looking accusingly from person to person. My brother said, "That's fucked up, man," and Curtis and I eagerly agreed. Rusty didn't look at me any differently than anyone else, but his stare was so incisive and angry, for a second he had me believing *I* had taken the coke. At nineteen, Rusty was three years older than me and he was big and burly and I couldn't imagine looking at him wrong let alone stealing drugs from him. Besides that, I wasn't the stealing kind. But Dilson was the kind and now he was hanging in the shadows like a hunted thing.

As I unlocked the car, Dilson and I heard the kitchen door slam. I quickly slid into the car and unlocked Dilson's door. Afraid that starting the car would attract attention, I slid the key into the ignition and asked Dilson what he wanted to do. Dilson looked around uneasily and then searched his belt for a hunting knife he had seated there. "Let's wait a minute." We sat in the dark and watched as whoever it was cast a shadow along the walls and across the ground. When the figure appeared in the parking lot, right off I could tell it wasn't Rusty. Too thin. A second or two later I recognized the gait and said "Curtis." He used his knuckle to rap on my window. I rolled it down and cigarette smoke emptied from the car. Curtis pulled off the hood to his sweatshirt and bent down, revealing his white-blonde flattop and strong nose.

"You shouldn't be here, Dil," he said.

Dilson shifted in his seat and looked straight ahead.

"I'm trying real hard not to be."

Curtis blew into his hands.

"Where you guys going?"

I looked at Dilson and when he didn't respond I said we were going to see Cleese.

"He still up in that mine living like a troll?"

I nodded that he was.

"Well fuck me running: drag him out of there. Tell him he can camp on our basement couch. Bron and May won't care."

Bron and May were Dilson and Curtis's parents and they had seen it all and they probably still are seeing it from what I hear. It was just the opposite with my own mother: As a single parent, she worked a full-time job and was therefore ignorant by virtue of absentia. I remember one of my brother's old girlfriends had run away from home and she had stayed at our house for over a month without my mother knowing about it.

"What do you say, D? Will you do that for me?" Curtis leaned in and looked directly at Dilson, who slapped the dashboard and said, "Let's go." I started the car and looked at Curtis.

"I'll give him the message," I said. "Do you want to come?"

"Not tonight, Buddy Boy." Then Curtis pulled on his hood and walked into the darkness.

He had only recently made a habit of retiring early. Having enlisted in the navy, which I suppose he saw as his chance to get his life together, he would be deploying in three months. I remember how excited he was to get on that boat and become a seaman. After he left, if I asked about him I might get snippets of information from Bron, but otherwise no one really talked about him. He was gone. Then one night about a year into Curtis's tour, over beers Dilson tells me he is coming home. "I thought he was in for a couple more years?" Dilson didn't have all the details, but he did know that during the Gulf War, Curtis's destroyer was a few hundred miles out in the Persian Gulf when the ship came under attack from above and below.

What was Curtis dreaming before the sirens ripped him from sleep and his wide eyes looked for boots and saw only his face and the December moon riding the heavy swells? How could he not feel the false hope of that sight? What did he make of his shipmates clamoring in the dark, their shouts and cries the death before the death, the blood ropes and air trails of drowning sailors racing into the unfathomable deeps?

"Thing is, it was just a drill," Dilson said, lighting a cigarette. He exhaled: "But he thought it was the real deal. Fight or flight, you know? But all that flew was his mind." Dilson made a bird with his hands and whistled as it flew away. "He got a medical discharge. His CO said it could have been worse," Dilson mused. "It's true. If he had died, it would have been worse. But I'll tell you what, when he got back, you'd think he'd dropped his brain on the floor."

Before we headed up to the mine, Dilson and I stopped at the 7-Eleven hoping to buy some smokes. Getting what we needed was always a task and a gamble. Luckily, the attendant was a large kid we called Koocher and he would sell us smokes and beer provided he was working alone and no other customers were in the store. That night I didn't have money for beer, but I had a hankering, so I went back to the cooler where the beer was kept and pulled a bottle from a six pack and guzzled it right there in the aisle. I went for another, but the bottle was wet with the cold and the son-of-a-bitch slipped out of my hand and shattered on the floor.

"What the fuck?" I heard Koocher say as he walked around the corner. I was standing there in a puddle of beer and broken glass with what was probably an *Oh, fuck, I'm busted* look on my face. To make matters worse, somehow I had managed to slice open my finger and my blood was dripping on the floor. I didn't even try to explain because it was so obvious and I didn't want to insult Koocher any more than I had already. "Are you okay?" he asked. I said I was and apologized and he said not to worry about it. I told Koocher I owed him big-time and then Dilson and I rounded up the smokes and three hotdogs with mustard and onions wrapped in foil and we left.

We drove east toward the mouth of the canyon, passed the polygamist compound, and then turned north and drove along the foothills and rounded a corner. We also passed the boulder field where three years later on a slick fall night my friends Wilkins and French would take the corner too fast on a motorcycle and rocket off the edge and into the field below. Wilkins was killed and French nearly so. I saw French a couple months after the accident and he still wasn't anywhere near right. I would not see him again. Nor did I see the point of attending Wilkins's funeral and so I never said goodbye. Months later, his death caught up with me and I cried hard for him. Lag time, I guess. Sometimes I think I should go out there and see if I can find Wilkins in the high yellow grass that hisses in the slightest wind. Or maybe in a drop of blood that fell someplace where the years could not wash it away. When the sun goes down, I change my mind. I tell myself he's not going anywhere.

I parked the car and Dilson and I scanned the mountainside for some sign of Cleese. There was no wind and as we stood there quietly and listened we heard rocks from the tailing slide and clack as Cleese dug his boots and tried to get a purchase on the stones. Then he appeared holding a can of blue flame. Dilson slung on his army/navy rucksack, lit a cigarette, and started up the old mining trail. I followed right behind him, but it wasn't long before he pulled away. When I got to the mine entrance, Dilson and Cleese had already gone in and I could hear them talking. I ducked into the mine and called out to them. Soon I saw a beam of light come flickering toward me. "Come this way," Cleese said as he shined the light a few feet in front of me. The golden dust hung in the air and the ground was damp from a seep.

After I reached him, Cleese pointed the light ahead and behind him so that we could both see as we walked down the tunnel and deeper into the mine.

"Where is your light?" Cleese asked.

"You're holding it."

I had explored this mine many years ago with my friend Deeg, my brother, and our dog, Gus, a husky/shepherd mix with soft floppy ears and a preference for squatting when he peed. When we came to a place I thought I recognized, I asked Cleese to stop and shine the light. The miners had tunneled about ten feet on either side of the main corridor and had formed a cross. When I was here last, I shined my light into one of the corridors and five or six white mice scattered among the rocks and small bones they had gathered. I'm not sure how well Gus could see in the pitch, but the instant my light hit those mice, he darted in there and snatched them up, one at a time, until they all lay broken and quivering or dead. He was a fine dog and he palled around with and protected us kids as if there were no greater purpose.

If we were the dominant group of kids in the neighborhood, he was the dominant dog and as such he fought a lot and in fact he killed my friend's dog, Kurt, a cranky old bastard who didn't realize how old and small he was compared to Gus. The general feeling was that Kurt had it coming. Five or six years later on a snowy December night Gus would have his own run-in with a car. Once things had ended between my mother and her fourth husband, Phil, we moved about a mile south of the neighborhood and Gus just couldn't let go of the old stomping grounds. Although we tried to discourage him, whenever Gus got the chance he would trek over there to check on things, I guess.

The travel through the neighborhoods was pretty safe, but to get from one neighborhood to the other, Gus had to cross 9400 South and he was not the first dog to have been killed along that road, nor would he be the last. One of the worst nights of my life was when my mother sat me down and told me he had been killed. In my life I've loved a few people who have died, but I loved that dog just as much, if not more.

When he saw me shine the light into the offshoot, Cleese asked me what I was looking for. "Mice," I said. "Now show me this armpit of the world you're so proud of." The end of the mine had been blasted out into a round room. Dilson was sitting on a pile of rocks and smoking coke out of a tinfoil pipe and the sweet, acrid smell of it mixed with the smell of burning candles that Cleese had placed on ledges around the room. I could see Dilson's bloodshot eyes and hear the sticky spittle in his mouth. "Is that for me?" I asked, gesturing toward a small mirror striped with several rills of coke. Dilson was still holding his hit, so he pointed to the mirror, nodded yes, and handed me a dollar bill.

I rolled the bill nice and tight and then snorted half the line up each nostril. I passed the bill and mirror to Cleese. Given his short and squat build, he seemed well suited for the tight quarters of the mine. As if he had evolved there. Once everyone was medicated, we lit cigarettes and drank Cleese's beer and talked about Rusty and how Dilson was going to get out of this self-made mess. My throat was numb and I could taste the blow's bitterness. I was in the middle of making some inane observation when my nose blood fell, went *splat*, and mingled with the dust on my boots.

I had to get some fresh air, so I took a candle and led myself out of the mine. I stood on the tailing and the fall wind blew out the candle and tore at my clothing and at my hair as the darkness spread out and gave way to the weak lights of the suburbs. To the south I could see the enormous granite boulder, like a big white house, and the drop in the ridgeline that signaled Bell Canyon Reservoir. A few nights before I visited Cleese in the mine, I went there with Tosser and Deeg. We were taking a walk up the old mining road when we came across the Egyptian's car and one other. "Bloody hell," Deeg said as the three of us stood there and from afar watched the Egyptian, her friend, and two boys we did not recognize. They were a good hundred yards up on the ridgeline, but they had built a nice fire and it lit them fully.

Incidentally, it was not unusual to hear American teens borrow expressions from across the pond or, worse, talk in an English accent for days at a time. But Deeg was from England so he could say it all with impunity. A true oddity, Deeg could not be invented. I knew him for about ten years and during that time he wore two hairstyles: a greasy bowl cut that he would comb forward and a menacing Mohawk arranged into seven ten-inch spires.

Like Curtis, Deeg had also joined the military but was later discharged after he was caught smoking dope. Unlike Curtis, he came back unscathed. The only thing different about him was that now he wore two military tattoos on each arm. Deeg was too defiant and aloof to be undone by something as predictable and regimented as everyday military life. Had he seen combat, things might have been different. Thinking about him now, it is hard to see how he was the product of his parents, so different were his features from theirs, especially his lips, which were very red and plump and suggestive. If anyone, he looked like his dad. In summer, Deeg's mom became an avid sunbather, and I remember how we kids were always happy to find her lying out in the backyard in her bikini.

Neither of his parents really trusted him and he spent many days up in his room like some demented British Rapunzel doing Lord knows what. Deeg wasn't allowed to drive, but he was happy to ride shotgun and I remember him arguing with a woman to whom we had lost a parking space in front of Koocher's 7-Eleven. I made the mistake of laughing and that incited him to call her a fucking cow in that heavy English accent of his and then he hissed at her like a cat with chocolate in its teeth. Deeg could be brutal. I think he had some redemptive qualities, although at this moment they escape me. He was funny. The last time I saw him was at my bachelor party in the White Mountains of eastern Arizona where, after a long weekend of heavy drinking in the woods, he snuck off and washed his ass in the stream.

When it came to sex, Tosser was an insatiable heat monster and he made no attempt to hide the fact. Several days before the fire-lit night in question, he had hooked up with the Egyptian's friend Charlene at a party, and once he knew she was up there on the mountain, boys or no boys, he was hell-bent on hiking up there and reclaiming his prize. I was feeling humiliated standing right where I was and I told him as much.

"I'm heading back," I said, and then I turned and started walking down the dirt road, kicking stones as I went and feeling a confusing combination of arousal, betrayal, and rage. Tosser pleaded with me, but to no avail. He hung back and watched the mountain for a couple of minutes and then followed me. Deeg was nowhere in sight. I asked Tosser about it and he said he saw Deeg snooping around the white truck that apparently belonged to the Egyptian's new male friends. We had made it to the mink farm above Tosser's house by the time Deeg caught up with us.

If most people exhale when they laugh, Deeg did just the opposite and brayed like a donkey. He had been running hard and he begged us to stop so he could catch his breath. If he weren't laughing, I might have kept going, but I knew he was laughing for a reason. In an act of malice and territoriality, he had crawled inside the white truck and shat on the front seat. If it were anyone else, I would not have believed it, but I knew Deeg either possessed or missed something that enabled him to cross the line between thinking and doing. He wasn't alone in

this, of course. We all did stupid and terrible things and I can't drive a
mile in any direction without reliving some of them. Midway through
life's journey, I am pressed between the barbs of the past and my fear
of the future.

★ ★ ★

I ducked back into the mine and lit the candle. Dilson and Cleese
were talking loudly and laughing. By then I had had my fill of the mine
and of the night. I was coming down and I could have gone up again,
but I heard their sticky white tongues and saw their bloodshot eyes set
adrift in their heads and I knew I was seeing myself and that nothing
good could come of the night. When I think about how my siblings
and I lived, and the dangers we exposed ourselves to, I must wonder
how we all made it to adulthood.

Now I think about my own kids and about the long road ahead
and how there are some things a mind cannot bear to contemplate.
How do people live with these shadowy possibilities? Sometimes I'll
flip through the obituaries and scan the pictures. I feel a little sadness
for the old folks, not because they have died, necessarily, but rather
because of how weathered and broken most of them look. I believe
this is why many of them pair recent pictures with much older ones,
as if to say *See? I was twenty once, too, and beautiful.* As if it mattered.
I know there is no escaping it. But when I see the babies and the children and the young men and women, the car I'm driving veers and
sails off the road, and suddenly life's randomness is almost impossible
to bear.

Then I think of those four kids—two girls, two boys—who, almost
two years ago to the day and an hour south of here, spent their last evening inside a mine, drowning.

I think about how those girls were so trusting of those boys, whom I imagine they had known since childhood, and how those boys must have felt like someone actually believed in them.

I never met them, but I know them and I miss them. I watch them there on the threshold, that point in time and space when a decision can still be reversed. But they are quiet, preparing, emptying their pockets of cell phones, cigarettes, matches, money, wallets. The older boy pulls off his T-shirt, sweeps back his hair and snaps it into a ponytail.

The girls notice his biceps, tattoos, dark bushy armpits, and rock-tit from the draft coming from somewhere deep in the mine. And maybe the younger girl, eighteen, remembers being in his arms as she looks outside and sees the sun setting.

The older boy says to expect total darkness. They will swim a twenty-foot tunnel to reach the small room deep inside the mine. *The tunnel is this big*, he says, making a circle with his arms. To avoid bunching up, everyone needs to count *one-one thousand, two one-thousand, three-one thousand* before following.

Everybody ready? he asks. *Shit yeah*, the other boy says, shaking out his arms and legs like a boxer before a fight.

The girls look at each other and smile weakly.

The first boy breathes deeply and on the count of three he disappears into the stagnant water. The other boy spits, says, *This is fucking sick, dudes.*

Their fates are joined as if by a rope that twists into the darkness.

The younger girl can't keep her eyes off the horizon. *I'm freaked*, she laughs, pulling off her socks, which resemble white roses after dark.

Inside the tunnel . . . clawing at the rank darkness, clutching, pulling himself through the murk, the older boy reaches the room, emerges, smells the black water . . .

Dead air . . . *Ohhhhh no* he whispers . . .

Just as the second boy rises—*Where are you?*

Here, the older boy hisses. *The air is bad . . .*

What?

Don't breathe.

The older girl is crushing her cigarette into the dirt and stepping into the water. *Don't worry, Sweetie.* Shoe soles flash and vanish.

One one-thousand, two one-thousand, three one-thousand.

PART THREE

CANINE TABLEAUX

KILL YOUR HEALTH AND KILL
YOURSELF, KILL EVERYTHING
YOU LOVE. AND IF YOU LIVE
YOU CAN FALL TO PIECES
AND SUFFER WITH MY GHOST.

—CHRIS CORNELL

I am looking at the only known, black-and-white photograph of my family. In it we are standing in what in life would be a yellow field near the house in Fort Fairfield. It is a clear, fall day in northern Maine. The wind is blowing from the west and the small white sun is shining in our eyes and all over our faces. Tall white grass is bending away and into the gray sky. My father is leaning against an old pasture fence and holding my sister on one side and on the other side my mother is standing with me and my brother. Someone could ride a horse through the space between them. My mother's hair is long and black and she has what could pass for a smile, but really her mouth is

91

squinting in the sun. Most of my father's face is hidden behind a heavy beard and thick waves of black hair. If they had thought to look hard at this photograph and acknowledge its emptiness, they might have seen beyond its time and place to the ruin it predicted.

If it is true that our dreams of the future stem from our experience of the past, when it comes to love and building enduring relationships, most of us probably have only ourselves to thank. I have never seen my parents touch each other even in friendship. I did see them touch other people. Does that count? When I was a kid living back east, my father slept upstairs and my mother slept down. My brother, sister, and I would visit my father and then commute down the stairs on an old mattress.

Although the Mormons were disapproving of this arrangement and would ultimately ostracize my mother because of it, to us kids it seemed perfectly natural because it was all we had ever known. But life together in that house had ended long before the Mormons came calling with their edicts: my parents lived together for the first eleven years of my life, but in all that time they never shared a bed.

Perhaps because of the intensity of their own mistreatment, in terms of their doctrinal zeal, eastern Mormons seemed more adamant about the need to live an upright life than their western counterparts. When they discovered my mother was no longer married to my father and he was still living with us, they called her into a meeting and later that winter a pair of them showed up at the door and presented her with a letter of excommunication. The two men were so resolute, they insisted on waiting there while she read the letter. God damn middle of winter and the wind is barging in and the precious wood heat is slipping out and those two pricks won't leave so she can close the door and start her new life.

★ ★ ★

Mother, mother, it's alright if you sleep with the flames tonight.

★ ★ ★

By April of 2006, Kim and I had been in Salt Lake City for a couple months and had bought the house in lower Mill Creek. We spent that spring and the better part of summer undoing the damage that had been done by time and by the previous owners, one of which was a Mormon metal worker who buried steel throughout the yard for reasons he took to his grave. While Kim worked upstairs, cleaning and painting and arranging, I demolished the basement until there was nothing left but concrete and the dusty guts and bones of the house. The work was filthy but good because it was cool down there and I needed something inconsequential to destroy.

From having spoken with Arlene, my neighbor to the east, I knew the metal worker had several children, including one boy whose stash of cigarettes, pipe tobacco, and women's underwear I found when I tore out the walls of his room. In another secret compartment he had a stack of smut magazines with comparatively benign titles like *Modern Man, Topper,* and *Gaze: Man-size Entertainment.* On the cover of *Topper* a blond, long-legged woman wearing heels, shorts, and a saffron blouse is bending over and preparing to hike a football. We can see her face, which is very red from being upside-down, but clearly her mostly covered bottom and legs are the focus. On the ground to her right, a helmet has been placed for additional context, and just in case there was any doubt this girl was a team player, which of course has nothing to do with playing football.

In the evenings, after the sun had dropped behind the trees and the yard was bathed in shadow, I would leave the basement and work outside, where I combed every inch of the yard, clearing it of steel, overgrowth, and debris that had amassed over the last fifty years. Like many Utahans who were around in the fifties, the original owners of our house had planted grape vines and raspberry bushes, as well as peach, pear, apple, and cherry trees, which they would harvest and can and enjoy throughout the year.

I spent rough hours cutting back ivy and silver lace that had spread throughout the trees and eclipsed their leaves just enough to keep them alive. Coddling moths had infested the apple tree and I would use my knife to dig the white larva from their holes even though I knew that it made no difference. The tree was as good as dead, but a pair of robins had made a nest in its dark center and in the evening when my work was done I would watch them through my son's window. Over the next few weeks, and for a few minutes each day, I watched as the birds grew the egg into a hatchling and the hatchling into a fledgling. One robin sat on the nest while the other hunted for insects and worms in the yard.

Because of how the robin tilts its head, I used to think it was listening for the worms, but in fact it was looking for them out of a single eye on either side of its head. After the robin yanked the worm from its hole, it cut it into strips and then flew it back to the nest, where the waiting chick chirped and flapped its fleshy wings as if it had never been fed. That spring and summer I slept with my bedroom window open for the cool sleeping weather and for the crickets' songs, and sometimes I would hear the chick's feeding sounds late at night and in my head I saw the chicks pecking at their parents who watched the darkness and did nothing to save themselves.

★ ★ ★

I knew I was dreaming when my mother asked me to go find my father and bring him home. The town where he had disappeared was somewhere in New England and it was empty and the streets were swept and wet with rain and the big windows of the diner where he sat were clean and dark so that I could not see through them. I was driving a big, black, heavy car made of steel and chrome that dated from the fifties. I floated to the curb, parked, and went inside.

My father sat in a booth of burled oak and red vinyl and he looked about twenty-five years old, which was my age at the time of the dream. He waved me over and I saw a glass of water in his hand. His other hand lay composed and with its fingers spread as if he were modeling rings. I sat down and he smiled at me, but it wasn't his smile, or if it was it was before my time. His hair was cropped neat and close and he wore a white oxford with a starched collar. I guessed he had just returned from Fire Island and, more recently, from the barber because his skin was very brown, clean shaven, and smelled like witch hazel.

Sitting a few booths down from us were two women with piled hair and an older man who wore a three-piece suit, the lapel of which was complemented by a corsage made from a species of flower that has not existed for ten thousand years. The older man looked at me and the blue veins in his forehead split and rose and reminded me of rivers seen from a great height. Then he turned and said something to the women, who then gazed at me demurely and laughed.

I was all bite and fire, and without really wanting to, I gave the man the finger, and it was as if a thundercloud had passed over his face. Afraid, I looked at the man who, by virtue of his age, could not yet be my father, but who was and would be still. The skin across his cheeks was tight and sunburned and it looked like his eyes had been embossed with delicate, white slashes that evoked the fossilized wings of a bird.

"Don't worry about them," he said haughtily. Then he got up and walked over to their booth. Where his hand had been there was a dirty human skeleton that was no bigger than a matchbox. My father sat with the women. A gruesome foursome, they were all laughing and their faces looked sweaty and demonic. The older man called to me, said, *Look, boy*, and lifted his sack and revealed a glowering orifice. *This is where the blood comes out.*

★ ★ ★

My fears slept so quietly, for years I believed they had been destroyed, that I had outgrown them. Now my children are here and I watch them grow strong even as I feel myself weaken in the season of the demon. When I am gone, who can say if their strength will be enough? When I was six years old, it took everything I had to hold my mother's hand and walk across the ice-crusted field behind our house. Our pregnant dog had wandered off into the storm. The wind whipped the loose snow into the air and, worried that we were lost, I looked back and tried to find the house. But it was gone in a way that only fire can make something gone.

And there we stood, smaller and weaker than the house and the storm that hid it. I peered up at my mother, the warrior, squinting at the blinding snow. Her mouth was shivering, or was she praying we wouldn't find that sweet girl and her litter of frozen pups? The essence of losing any living thing is that we cannot say if it's alive or dead and that uncertainty works on the imagination until it resembles an empty grave. And nothing raises questions like an empty grave unless it includes an annotated copy of the *Duino Elegies* and it is circled by the footprints of a child.

Winter and spring storms had come and gone in Maine and at the end of the wet season, my mother, father, and us kids moved to another town where nothing really happened in the open. Farmers drove tractors down the street and teenagers peeled their tires in the Burger Boy parking lot and that was something. Once in a while the gray bird of death would soar through town and announce someone had died. Maybe an old guy fixing the roof after a rain. Mindful of the black clouds far down the sky, he raises his hammer and the lightning strikes it. Out of the corner of his eye he watches the crystal flame leap to his head, where it burns a tiny hole and then travels the roads of his bones and blows his boot soles clean off.

Down at the diner, folks sit next to their hats and purses, eat pancakes and eggs, and drink their coffee. They reason one's got to be smarter than the lightning or whatever did the killing and suddenly made life feel broken and not necessarily in a bad way. Country life in Aroostook County got to be monotonous, so my brother, sister, and I were pretty excited and a little afraid when a young man on a motorcycle lost his leg when he was sideswiped by a car. Actually he didn't lose his leg: It was laying there next to him. Bad luck is hard to take because it explains a lot, but it has no use for anything it claims.

I knew the man that hit him. His name was Duff. I went to school with his son and he told me it was hard to see how the accident had affected his dad because he would smile sometimes and was still standing. Without invitation he reminded me how two summers before a fire had destroyed my family's barn, but not a lick of flame had touched the adjoining house. I didn't know what to think because this same kid had also told me his older brother had kooky eyes and talked as if he had to spit because he had goofed off and accidentally driven a pencil into his ear.

My brother, sister, and I watched the ambulance come screaming up the road and as it passed everyone's hair went flying. We then walked half a mile to have a look. Duff and the motorcyclist were gone, but we saw the wreckage. The motorcycle lay smoking in the road. In a state of shock, the man didn't realize he was minus one leg and tried to run across the grass without it, and we judged he did not get far. Then Duff must have sat him down on the gutter because there was a pool of arterial blood there that seeped into the storm drain. The pool had started to congeal around the edges, but the center was still wet and alive in the evening sunlight, and it became a dark mirror in which I saw two faces. My advice is to pass the closed doors found in dreams and in a pool of a stranger's blood. My advice is to keep walking.

★ ★ ★

After work I walk across campus and into the January wind with my head down. Last autumn's leaves and a torn page of math notes lay trapped and shining beneath the ice. When I look up I see a young woman and I think I am seeing my two-year-old daughter, Greer, sixteen years from now. I wonder if she knows the beauty and the danger inside her and inside young men and in the men who do not reveal themselves; I worry about the strength of their hands and their smiles like glass hidden by the summer grass; and about all the deadly and blazing animals leaping aghast out of the moonless night and places too far from here, where the world is a lightless betrayal and goes by unnoticed. I want to take that girl by the arm and sit her down and make her promise she'll take care for as long as I am here and long after.

Over dinner I tell Kim I saw Greer as a teenager and what it did to me and she tells me she does the same thing all the time. I want to believe we are sharing and feeling this together, but I can't be sure. I say, *If I can just make it to seventy, the kids will be in their thirties and by then they should be alright.* I feel like I have it figured out, like I will have done my job and fulfilled my obligations, but then I look at Kim and she is spinning her fork in the noodles and looking at her plate. *That's not so much the issue for me. I think about how much of their lives I am going to miss.* I'm afraid she is right.

Now here is this new void created by contemplating my children's parentless lives. I get up and carry our plates to the sink. When I return I stand behind Kim and put my hands on her shoulders. The hard ridges of her collar bones feel unfamiliar and sadness and fear creep into my heart. I want to say something about the intersection of time and desire and how we chose this. But then Wilder asks us what we're talking about, and as is our habit, at the exact same moment Kim and I say, *Nothing.*

Becoming a parent is a complicated experience. Such strangeness and emptiness in the fact that Kim and I will be erased from the Earth except for our children's memories, which too will fade and conclude by their own erasure. Impermanence makes the blood flutter. Life widens from its beginning until its end. Everything else is dissolution. I am unsettled by the paradox promised by the birth of each child.

I have this image of Kim and our kids lying in bed. Greer nurses and Wilder describes a yucky dream. Kim pushes the hair off his forehead, which is hot because he has been crying. They don't know it, but I am on the floor beside the bed. I am out of sight and in another world. I see myself searching my pockets for matches. When I don't find any, I feel relieved because it means that I don't have to go through with this, and that I *can't.* And I am just about to rise and climb in to bed when Kim's arm falls out of the sheets, and in her hand is a book of matches. The window is open. Above the wind we hear the dark songs of robins and ruined apples falling on the roof.

After dinner, Wilder brings me his children's book about endangered animals and we see all the species whose days are numbered. Then we come to the chapter about extinction: Wilder points to the vivid pictures of the dodo, Tasmanian tiger, and Steller's sea cow. He wants to know where they live and what they do. I say *nowhere* and *nothing*. Extinction is absence multiplied to the trillionth power: it is a billion years of emptiness. It is the stone that will not reach the bottom of the well. But we were sharing each other's warmth, sitting on a soft red couch with a blanket across our legs. The house is clean, warm, and well lit. It is snowing again. Big white flakes. Light snow. Greer is at the kitchen table talking to frozen blueberries. Her face and little hands are stained with the juice. Kim is slicing tomatoes, avocado, feta cheese, and bread and arranging them with shavings of prosciutto ham. Olive oil glistens in small white bowls.

I want to hold someone's head in my hands and say *I am grateful* and *I do not want this to end*. But there is no one to tell. Tonight the wind presses against the door and the windows bow. *These are the most important years of your life and you're squandering them on fear. Your quiet moments are the most insane.* I hear this other voice and I think, *Yes, yes*. The wind is moving in the heavy branches of the old blue spruce and I wonder *Will it fall and crush us in our sleep?* The wind says things in different ways. It drones and hisses: *Step aside, wolf spider. This house is full of cracks. I found a way inside. Do you hear that mournful sound?* The children breathe slow and deep in the December air.

★ ★ ★

On the playground today, a little boy struck my son in the neck and the killer inside me opened his eyes.

★ ★ ★

No yucky dreams tonight,
no yucky dreams tonight,
no yucky dreams tonight;
only sweet dreams,
only sweet dreams,
only sweet dreams.

★ ★ ★

A flock of starlings swirling into the freezing air above the cemetery is my choice of metaphor for the women I have known. One was
the Egyptian. I lived inside her the way I lived inside certain houses
whose rooms I misremember. *Was the bed against that wall? Wasn't
there a picture hanging here? Has that window always been broken?*
I do know the Egyptian was two years older than me and was well
versed in coitus and amorous madness by the time she rode bareback
into Utah. While our Mormon counterparts were engaged in wholesome play and hand-holding, the Egyptian and I had become expert
in alcohol consumption and in the acts it enabled us to perform with
abandon. And in this endeavor we were joined by several others who,
so it seemed, were satellites orbiting the craziest of the crazies. This
was long before the days of Lark. I cut my teeth on the Egyptian. The
booze made it easier to indulge our curiosity about each other's geni-
tals, those mysterious and pungent loci of all desire. Alcohol opened a
door—many doors, actually—that would not have opened otherwise
or at least not without real effort.

Opening any door under any circumstance is always a gamble,
mind you. Especially if there is an angry person on the other side of
it, or if it is hot and smoke is curling beneath it. But if behind the door
there was a beautiful girl holding a six-pack, I would happily take my

chances. That's the thing, though: until I opened the door, I couldn't know what awaited me. Nor could anyone, not even the Mormon kids, whose eyes were clear and glazed with a kind of acquiescence and inexplicable certainty. What desires would awaken inside them? I want Wilder and Greer to see this. I want them to know how risky and beautiful and unnecessary it is to open doors sooner than later. If I had known I was bound to open those doors anyway—and maybe I wasn't—then I would say it was better to be done with it. To be done with the Egyptian. Toward the end, we were a violent and sexual conflagration of saliva and gasoline. We combusted.

Before that time, though, the Egyptian was my eighteen-year-old professor and I was her attentive, sixteen-year-old student. She was gracious enough to offer her bedroom as a classroom and her body as a teaching instrument. She was a proponent of the hands-on approach to instruction, in which case she would take my hand and put it in important places, sort of like how you might put a finger on an important passage in a text.

In addition to acquainting me with female anatomy, the Egyptian also helped me to refine my skills as a wrestler. The Egyptian and I loved to wrestle. In fact, we wrestled with such fervor that the moment we would meet we would get down into the wrestling position known as *Advantage/top*, with her on the bottom and me on top. Anyone observing us from space or by hidden camera or through an open window would have been caught up in the excitement of our match. Of course, there came a day when the wrestling match no longer sufficed as an outlet for our feelings toward each other.

On this day we had been lying out in the sun, and what would turn out to be our final wrestling match commenced when we came inside to cool off and eat some bologna, cheese, and lettuce rolls, which was the only thing the Egyptian was willing to make. The colonel and the Egyptian's mother were at work, so the Egyptian suggested we take a cold shower and wash each other. She had sweet-smelling soaps and soft luffas, and the washing part sounded nice, but I had been a supervisor at a tanning salon and in one of the few instances where I actually knew something for sure, I told her that we should skip the shower if we intended to keep our suntans. She looked doubtful, so I mentioned melanin cooling prematurely and we made a beeline for the basement, which was the coolest place in the house and the Egyptian's refuge from her annoying little brother and intrusive parents.

She dived onto the bed and I dived onto her and the match commenced. I had a good hold on her from behind, but the Egyptian had recently applied a generous helping of suntan oil, and in that slippery state she easily freed herself from my grasp. After several failed attempts, I pinned her on her bed, a process that required me to lie between her legs—her center of gravity—and press down with my pelvis. She laughed and wiggled beneath me and that just made me press down harder. I was about to blow, which would have been embarrassing, so I slid off of her and to settle down I thought about dirt floors and sewage and any ugly son-of-a-bitch that came to mind. That's when Koocher and a couple of my friends appeared and I said, *Okay, fellas, you did your part. Now get the fuck out of here.*

Next thing I know I'm kissing the Egyptian and our tongues are laying together and she tastes like coconut oil and bubble gum. We passed the gum back and forth. It was fresh and warm and I enjoyed it. I can't speak for her, but I think it kept me from eating her tongue. Sometimes when I was drunk and I closed my eyes in the dark and kissed the Egyptian, I would forget my body. As if I were a head with a mouth and tongue, the rest of me had been made of sand and, wave upon wave, it had washed away. But that pleasure never lasted long. If I started spinning, I would put one foot on the floor like an anchor and try to focus on a single object: one of my shoes, the Egyptian's bikini bottoms, the basket overflowing with spent cans of hair spray. None of it ever worked. If he were alive, my grandfather would say I was trying to fix a leaky roof with a broken hammer.

At sixteen, I was sorely ill-equipped to cope with loss of any kind, especially the loss of my first lover. So now, a quarter-century later, I understand why I fell apart and broke what I could of the world around me when I learned the Egyptian was moving away. A few days before she left, we had a small going-away party at her house and it felt like a strange, desperate, and last-ditch attempt at happiness if only because the house—four walls and a roof—was empty except for beds and a few boxes. Earlier that evening, Brody picked me up in his Monte Carlo, a hideous boat with *Porsche Eater* stenciled with black electrical tape across the trunk. This was Brody's not-so-subtle way of alerting suburbia, and the yuppies who populated it, to the beast beneath the hood: a 454, high-performance race engine.

That car rumbled like a thunderstorm when it idled, and it idled a lot lest it not have sufficient fuel to devour challengers. I lived at the bottom of the street and Brody would coast down it and then rub up next to the curb, like a fat cat rubs up against your legs, and honk the horn. Brody was generally shy in social situations, but when it came to the piloting of vehicles—bikes, motorcycles, cars—he was without question the most assertive and adroit operator I have ever known. Unlike Tosser, who was notorious for his terrible judgment behind the wheel, and who had damn near killed me at least two times that I can remember, Brody knew how to control the vehicles he operated and I trusted him.

When I got outside I could hear punk rock coming from the Monte and I saw my other friend Dirtbag riding shotgun and playing drums on the dashboard, his longish brown hair lashing as he did so. As I approached, he swung open the huge door and leaned forward so I could tilt up the seat and climb in the back.

"How's it hangin'?" I asked, sliding into the car. Next to me was an open case of Pabst Blue Ribbon. "Hello, beautiful," I said, popping open a beer. Before I drank, I sank down into the seat and out of sight. Dirtbag twisted around and looked back at me:

"Courtesy of Koocher," he said with the same smile he's been smiling his whole life.

"Koocher's a good man. How do, Brody Alamode?"

Brody looked at me in the rearview. Back then his eyes were still clear and bright and playful.

"Just trying to keep the fucking Priottzo under control." He gestured toward Dirtbag who, like himself, had at least two different aliases.

I was present the night he was dubbed "Priottzo." Our friend Reed's grandmother had a nice swimming pool on the east side of town, and one night when she was away on business, Reed hosted a party at her house. Most of the revelers were happy to sit poolside and drink a few beers, but Dirtbag, who was boisterous and playful, took off all his clothes, grabbed some beers, climbed up a tree, and got up on the roof. The pool lights bathed everything in a turquoise light. As if a piece of the moon had fallen into the water.

After he had pounded a couple beers, Dirtbag walked down to the edge of the roof and stood there laughing. He was very muscular and I guessed if I had his body I would be up there, too. The girls giggled and the boys laughed and heckled him, but no one turned away from the great, hairless ape. Then Dirtbag grabbed his package and shook it at the world below him. "The Priottzo laughs at you!" he yelled as he jumped into the pool, his prick slapping the water.

Brody put the Monte in drive and the big car rumbled out into the street.

"Fucking Priottzo," I said, looking at Dirtbag and remembering his rooftop antics. "Let's get out of here before my mom gets home."

Brody punched the accelerator and we raced up the hill.

"Slow down," I said.

Dirtbag wiped beer from his pant leg. We were going so fast and the hill was so steep that I was sure we were going to rocket into the air and leave the planet, which wouldn't have made any sense because everything we wanted was right here. Then Brody decelerated just as we reached the top of the hill and gravity took over. Everything falls back to the Earth.

The Egyptian's house was not even a mile away from my own, and I remember walking to or away from there many times in the early morning hours and looking at the blackness of the night above me and smelling the sweet sage of the desert, which at the time was never very far. Truth is, I could have walked backward with my eyes closed to the Egyptian's house. I had counted the steps and I knew the roads by their sounds—dogs and chimes, mostly—and whether the wind blew down them.

"Where are we going?" I asked when Brody turned right instead of left.

"Nose candy!" Dirtbag answered, gleefully.

"Fuck, from where?" I asked.

Brody hawked some phlegm and spat out the window: "From the Hippie," he said, annoyed. "Don't worry, we have plenty of time."

But I wasn't worried about being late. I hated going on drug runs. "I'm not going in there," I said, knowing I was only in slightly less danger sitting in the car than being inside. Apart from my general anxiousness, I didn't care for the Hippie or his shithole apartment. He was an angry drunk and a thirty-year-old loser whose part-time occupation was selling drugs to kids like us.

However much I may or may not have enjoyed chemicals, I didn't want anything to do with getting them, and I detested drug culture and the people who acted as if being incoherent were something to be proud of. I mean, go ahead, drink or snort or smoke until you're a hundred miles away, but for Christ's sake, don't act all proud of the fact. Were it not for my friends, some of whom seemed less concerned with appearances, I doubt anyone would have suspected me, a clean-cut, mild-mannered kid from the burbs. And that is how I wanted it.

As early teens, we were not yet full-fledged losers, so I could still look at someone like the Hippie, or at my own brother's room—a veritable shrine to grass—and know that I didn't want that life. But as of the day we pulled up to the Hippie's apartment to score some blow, I was almost a decade away from fully realizing my aversion to drug culture and from giving up that slow death.

Dirtbag and I waited in the car while Brody got out and walked up to the door. A few seconds later the door opened a crack and Brody looked back at us and then walked inside. The curtain opened a little and I saw the Hippie peering out at us.

"What a fucking dick," I said.

Dirtbag was rolling a cigarette.

"Who, the Hippie?"

"Who else?" I asked.

"He's harmless," Dirtbag laughed, putting the final licks on his cigarette.

"You shouldn't roll those things in public. A cop sees that shit and we're screwed," I said, looking out the windows to see if anyone saw us.

Dirtbag lit the cigarette, turned around and looked at me. "You worry too much."

"Yeah, well, I don't want to get busted . . . and he's not harmless."

Later, Brody and the Hippie would share an apartment on the west side and we partied there pretty hard and regularly and would have indefinitely had Brody not lost his mind one night in a fit of jealous paranoia. J-Bird and Bay were girl friends of ours from school and Bay and Brody had dated once. I had also dated Bay a couple years before, but we did not last long once the Egyptian appeared on the scene. She was like that character in the movies who gallops by and reaches for someone on foot and then swings him onto the back of the horse and they ride away.

The last night we partied at Brody's apartment, J-Bird and Bay were in Brody's room deciding whether or not to kiss and I was in the bathroom. When I came out, the Hippie had just returned home to find Brody having a tantrum. *What's wrong, Brody?* I asked, buzzed and confused. But Brody didn't answer, and instead he went into his room, kicked out J-Bird and Bay, and slammed the door.

When I tried to go in and talk to him, the Hippie intervened and grabbed me by the arm and yelled at me to leave him the fuck alone or he was going to kick my ass out of there. I said, "Shit, I'll save you the trouble." Then I left. A few days later I called Bay and she told me the reason Brody freaked was because he thought I was getting it on with her and J-Bird in his room. I'd known Brody for a long time and we were good friends, but even the strongest male relationships don't have much of a chance when there's a pretty girl in the picture, let alone *two* of them.

Dirtbag blew a big hit of blue smoke into the windshield. "The Hippie is a fucking pussy, man. You could take him," he said, dismissively.

I looked outside and saw Brody walking toward the car.

"Maybe so," I said.

The Hippie was a lot taller than me and even if I got lucky and was able to punch him in the sack, I would still likely pay a heavy price. *Fuck that*, I thought. I had seen *Rocky* five times and I knew what a good punch could do to a face. I didn't need any rearranging courtesy of the Hippie or anyone else. For what it was worth, I appreciated Dirtbag's faith in me, but I also knew it was mostly his faith in himself. The Hippie really was a pussy from his perspective. Dirtbag was super strong, muscular, and aggressive. Add that to the fact he didn't really give two shits if he got hit, and that made him one dangerous SOB. When he fought, he was a berserker if there ever was one.

Brody got into the car and seemed very pleased with his purchase. "Hand me a beer," he said.

I pulled out a beer and passed it between the seats. When Brody started the car, the music came on again and he turned it down so he could hear the engine. Apparently satisfied by what he did or did not hear, he put the car in gear and we floated into the street and into the wider sea of the Hippie's alien suburb. As we drove out of there, I recalled one winter night when we were leaving the Hippie's and we got into bad blood with some other kids when they cut us off.

The incident should have come and gone, but Reed, who was tall, gangly, and fearless, was in the mood for mischief and things escalated from there. We were in his turbo Saab and the other kids were driving some American shit that we could have dusted right then and there if we had so chosen. Reed would not let it go, though, and he slipped out a small bat and lamely struck the other car as we passed it. Brody was riding shotgun and he laughed like a maniacal cherub and shouted genital profanities at the other car's occupants. I was in the back trying to keep tabs on my cohorts while at the same watching the other car.

I could see there were about six of them. Then I saw shiny steel winking through the darkness. I put my hand on Reed's shoulder and leaned forward.

"I counted six of those fuckers, and I think they're packing," I said.

Brody didn't want it to end, and he took his half-empty beer can and lobbed it out the window and over Reed's car like a grenade. He timed it badly and it sailed off and landed in someone's yard. "Fuck it all!" he yelled.

I could feel it. Time was running out. Something had to change, and fast. "Let's lose these pricks," I said. And as if I had flipped a switch, Reed shifted down into second gear and punched the gas. We quickly pulled away and I watched the other car dissolve into the soup of smog and shadows. Brody blasted the radio and pounded another beer. Reed's hands were in the nine and three positions on the wheel and he stared ahead, unblinking, as if he were in a trance.

As I watched him negotiate the road, I realized he was driving to the rhythm of the song and he drove beautifully. He was doing *The Reefer*, which was a dance he created that allowed him to move like a wave without moving his legs, except now he was dancing with the car as it barreled through the night. He was wrecked on blow and beer and by that means he had somehow merged with the mind of the car. It was slightly magical. A couple of minutes later, the other car was long gone, but Reed was still melded and his eyes were glassy with synthetic happiness. I was about to feel happy myself. But then his eyes widened and we spun around and off the road.

When we finally stopped, I sat up and looked around. The car had stalled and all I could hear was the *tink tink tink* of the engine. "Did we hit ice?" I asked, wiping the dew from the back window. Now that we were still and quiet and the lights were off, I noticed the heavy, yellow smog that had settled into the valley. I didn't know where we were, but I did not want to be there.

"Let's fucking blaze, Reed," I said. "Start the car." Reed took the car out of gear and put his hand on the key, but he didn't turn it.

"Let's have a beer first," he said.

"Dude, what if they come?"

"Be cool, man," he said, cracking a beer.

I looked at Brody, hoping he would say something. But all I saw was that empty winter field of my childhood.

When Brody, Dirtbag, and I finally got to the Egyptian's house for the going-away party, she was outside on her front porch. "Park that leaky boat on the street!" she yelled, referring to the Monte's constant oil leak. She, J-Bird, and Bay sat barefooted and were smoking cigarettes and drinking wine coolers out of Big Gulp cups. Donning their makeup and motley garb, they could have been doubles for the Material Girl in various stages of intoxication.

They were beautiful girls with an outrageous hair style known as the *claw,* which could be imitated by touching the wrist to the forehead with the hand palm out and fingers spread; and this is exactly what Dirtbag did as we approached the inebriated vixens. "Grrrrrrr!" he laughed. "You're an anus," Bay said, and the Egyptian and J-Bird agreed. Whenever the Egyptian got really sauced, her eyes got wet and lazy and they were that way now. I could see I had some catching up to do if I intended to relate. This was late summer and so the days were long and we could get pie-eyed drunk before the sun went down.

But when the sun finally did go, the crickets sang and the sprinklers hissed in the grass and life in the burbs became this sweet and mindless thing we all loved without knowing it. And sometimes in moments as brief as those between these words we would sit in the yard or in the empty rooms with the windows open and know the warm, desert wind was blowing down the roads and through the fence slats, and that nothing could stop it.

By dark we were inside and in various states of disrepair. The Egyptian, Bay, and J-Bird were sitting on the floor with their backs against the wall, since there was no furniture, gossiping and feeling so sorry (*but not really*) for the girl at school who bled through her white jeans on the school bus. The Egyptian was three years older than the other two girls, and next to her J-Bird and Bay looked like huge dolls that were being played with by unseen hands. Compared to the Egyptian, who was complicated by her past and had this air about her that reminded me of a meadow in which people had been killed, J-Bird and Bay were fairly wholesome and had opposite simplicities that appealed to me and that I sought to possess.

Brody had been outside fiddling with the Monte, and when he came inside his hands and forearms were slathered with heavy grease. He also now had a grease Hitler mustache that he had apparently grown when he scratched his upper lip with his greasy finger. "You look fucking ridiculous!" Dirtbag said. And he really did, but I didn't laugh because I have an unusual sense of humor. I think this is funny:

It is a sunny day and an old barber has just swept out his shop. He decides to take a break on the stoop, and as he is standing there leaning on his broom, enjoying the shade and the sights and sounds of the neighborhood, a young girl eating a cookie comes walking down the street. Just as she passes the barber shop, the girl accidentally drops her cookie on the sidewalk. "Oh, little girl, did you get hair on your cookie?" the barber asks, clearly concerned. The girl looks up at him and says "Jesus Christ, mister, I'm only ten years old!"

Back at the Egyptian's, the girls started laughing like demonic, hot-faced clowns at Brody's mustache. He didn't seem to care either way and when he left the room to wash I figured the girls would shut their cake-holes and would move on to something else, and so I was happy for a moment. I should have known better, though, because this was all there ever was when we were drinking; there was nothing to move on to; and that sure as shit wasn't going to change now, on the night of the Egyptian's last hoorah.

Eventually everyone except for the Egyptian stopped laughing and I could hear the music again:

> What happened to you?
> You're not the same.
> There's something in your head
> That's made a violent change . . .
> It's in your head, it's in your head . . . filler.
> You call it religion, you're full of shit.

Minor Threat was one of my favorite bands and normally I'd be singing along at the top of my lungs, but all I could hear was the Egyptian's drunken laughter and it filled me with rage. I attribute about 3 percent of that rage to the fact that she was laughing at Brody and humiliating him. But the other 97 percent came from the fact that a huge part of my world had been sheared off and was drifting into space and here she was, completely beside herself with drunken mirth. How could she laugh *at all,* let alone so uncontrollably and with such relish? "What's so fucking funny?" I asked, standing above the Egyptian.

Apparently she did not like my tone or my intrusion into her personal space and she told me to fuck off as she pushed herself up the wall and went outside to smoke a cigarette. "Fuck off? Fuck you," I said, at my inarticulate best. I wasn't finished venting, but I was stupid with alcohol. Then she started laughing again and I checked out, smashed through the guard rail, and went flying over the edge.

I followed her outside and threw her down on the ground with more force than I had expected. I knew I had fucked up major. But I didn't get to think about it because Dirtbag and Brody tackled me and pinned me to the ground. I felt the wet grass and saw an earthworm slide into its hole.

"You're out of control, man," Dirtbag said with restrained anger, as if at any moment he might also lose control and rain down hell on me.

"Okay, I know. Just let me get up and get out of here," I said, breathing heavily and in that weird baying voice that precedes crying. When I got up, the Egyptian was gone, spirited away by J-Bird and Bay.

I walked home with the wind at my back. Whenever I saw the headlights of approaching cars, afraid they might be cops, I would duck out of sight and wait for them to pass. Once, after I had just begun my wait, I felt something watching me. I looked to my right and, peering through a broken fence slat was the star-white face of a husky/wolf mix. It didn't move or make a sound. It just stood there, watching me, reversing a curse.

When I got home the house was dark, it was midnight, and I was far from sleep. I got into my car and drove toward the Egyptian's house. I parked a block away, perhaps to give myself time to figure out what I was going to do. I did not know why I was there. Bay's car was in the driveway. I leapt the fence like a cat and dropped into the backyard, where I would have access to the Egyptian's basement window. I knelt in the dirt and looked inside and saw Bay lying alone in the Egyptian's king-sized bed, talking to someone who was not in the room. My shoes reeked.

Knowing the Egyptian was hiding somewhere in the basement, I rapped on the glass. Bay startled, pushed off the sheet and came to the window. Even now that we were just friends, I felt like she still loved me and would do anything for me, including betray one of her best friends. She had big brown fawn eyes with which she rarely made eye contact. "Where is she?" I asked. Bay looked me in the eye and said she did not know where the Egyptian had gone. If there was any doubt the Egyptian was there, Bay dispelled it when she looked me in the eye: I had slept with her, so I knew when she was lying. But I played along and asked if I could come inside and wait and see if the Egyptian returned. Bay said I could, so I jumped into the window-well and climbed down into the room.

The moment my feet landed on the floor, my uncertainty about why I was there vanished. I was there to hunt. Perhaps Bay expected me to sit quietly on the bed, but I immediately began searching the adjoining rooms, talking menacingly as I did so. "So, she's not here," I mused. "I wonder where she could be? Come out, come out wherever you are. Ollie Ollie in come free." I glanced at Bay and she was sitting straight up in bed with a wild expression on her face. "Am I getting warmer?" I asked. I knew my quarry was close because I could smell her hair spray and the makeup on her face. I walked around the water heater and the Egyptian made a break for it. That triggered my capture instinct and I pounced on her and pinned her to the floor.

"I'll strangle the life out of you," I said as I placed my hands around her throat. I didn't squeeze, though, because I couldn't believe what I had just said. It was like I was speaking a line from a made-for-television teenage drama. I was playing the part of the troubled teen from a broken home and with a drinking problem. Of course all this was lost on the Egyptian, who looked up at me with this silly, terrified look on her face. By then Bay had come into the room and was screaming at me to get off the Egyptian. *What the fuck am I doing here?*

I had broken things beyond repair and I was going to be in serious trouble if the Egyptian told anyone about what must have seemed like an attempt on her life. In my adrenaline- and alcohol-soaked fog, I let the Egyptian get away before I could make her understand I was sorry. She wasn't going to stick around to find out how Lenny handles the rabbit because she already knew. I could hear her crying as she ran up the stairs, and then the house was silent. Again my pursuit instinct kicked in, except this time the motivation was panic. When I didn't find her on the ground-level floor, I ran upstairs, frantically, pathetically, apologetically calling her name.

I opened the door to the guest bedroom and was elated when I saw her lying in the bed. I rushed over to her and shook her wildly. I had spoken her name the third time when I realized it wasn't the Egyptian I had awakened, but the colonel, who must have come home after I had left the first time.

"What the fuck?" I whispered.

"What in the Sam-hell are you doing?" the colonel asked, sleepily.

"Oh shit, colonel, I'm sorry." Then I turned and ran and I did not stop. The Egyptian wouldn't leave for a few more days, but as of that night she was gone and gone for good.

★ ★ ★

Right before bed last night, Wilder saw his shadow on the wall and he said, "Love you, shadow."

★ ★ ★

The spring of the year following the Egyptian's departure, Brody, J-Bird, Bay, and I drove through the then horse town of Draper, Utah, which is where Bay and J-Bird lived. We had some time to kill before we went night swimming at a friend's house just outside of town. When Brody's hand was not on the gear shift, it was entwined in Bay's hand. Brody would eventually sabotage their relationship, but for now their hands were clamped together in the front seat and J-Bird and I sat in the back. One thing that has not changed about the Salt Lake Valley is that it gets plenty of sleep at night. Rural areas like Draper felt like they never did awaken. That night we drove the speed limit toward Corner Canyon and it was a strange night because we could feel spring and we were sober.

Brody could no longer afford the Monte and he had since gotten a VW Bug. J-Bird and I had been friends and we liked and were comfortable with one another and I remember it was easy to be with her in such a small space as that. As we neared the foothills, a cat darted out into the road and under the tire. "Oh, fuck!" Brody yelled. J-Bird and I had not seen it happen, but we felt the bump. Bay was freaking out and bitching at Brody who, at J-Bird's suggestion, swung onto the shoulder and turned around.

As we headed toward our unfortunate victim, we saw another cat sitting not even a foot away from the squished cat. I was waiting for the cat to bolt at the sound of the car, but we pulled up to within fifteen feet and it didn't move. It just sat there and looked at the other cat with unblinking intensity. We could all see the dead cat was without collar, in which case there was nothing to be done. I am a cat lover, though, so I volunteered to move the cat from the road. Another car likely wouldn't pass through there until noon of the next day, but I decided that didn't matter. When the other cat saw me coming it rose and walked into the darkness. "Motherfuck," I said, looking down at the cat. Its brain had popped out of its mouth and its face was flat and empty like a skinned animal's.

I looked back at the car, but the high beams were on and I couldn't see jack. I grabbed the cat by the tail and pulled it onto the side of the road. I made sure the cat wasn't hidden so it would be found should someone come looking for it. That person would see the drag trail of organs, bone, and blood painted out to the center of the road and that knowledge would change absolutely nothing.

I asked for a cigarette when I got back in the car, and Brody drove us out of there. We didn't talk much for the next while and when we got to the foothills, Brody and Bay wandered off in one direction and by default J-Bird and I went in another. I could sense the soft earth underfoot but the high grass that had lain dormant under the heavy snow for months kept us atop it. J-Bird and I found a thick tuft and we sat and shared a clove cigarette, which had become a kind of delicacy since their sale had been outlawed in Utah after a kid in California died from smoking them and the autopsy revealed over a dozen cists the size of golf balls in his stomach. I thought about that kid and how it must suck to be dead as the wind came out of the south and carried the smoke away from our mouths and out into the quiet night. J-Bird leaned into me when the wind gusted and we both ducked our heads to the north and laughed and I could smell and feel her hair blowing across my face. She was a very sweet and playful girl with high cheekbones and a sultry smile, so being anywhere near her was very nice.

When the warmish wind died we would look up again and gaze to the south, as if we expected to see something other than the black shapes of the rising mountains. We could see Bay and Brody silhouetted against the northern sky and their bodies were stiff and serious. Bay's arms were folded. I think everyone knew they wouldn't last. It wasn't just them, though. We all had potential, but we lost most of it to the drugs and booze and to the resulting mistakes, which made me feel like I was always in the hole. Add that to the normal difficulty of interacting with other humans, and how any of us got and stayed together with anyone could be counted as one of life's mysteries.

Eventually Bay walked down the hill with her arms folded and Brody sat on the side of the mountain and watched her go. I turned to J-Bird and told her I'd meet her down at the car and she smiled and said, "See you there, underwear." I cut up the side of the mountain to where Brody was sitting and his face looked pale and smooth like the face of child. At my approach he opened his eyes and looked at me and blinked.

"She hates me," he said.

I knew that was as close as Brody would get to asking me for help. "Don't worry," I said, offering a hand. "She'll come around."

"I don't think so," he said, lighting a cigarette. And neither did I.

The pool was indoors and belonged to a girl I'll call "Faux." She came from a Mormon family that was so big, I never did get a full head count. Her parents were older by any measure and whenever I

glimpsed them passing by the windows I would think thoughts like
Why did you have so many goddamn kids? and *You don't have a fucking
clue about what's going on out here, do you? That's okay,* I'd think. *Stay
in the dark so I can finish my beer and my buddy can grope your daughter in peace.* And other times, if I were feeling friendly, I'd wish Faux's
mom would bring us some of those delicious Mormon eats, but that
never happened.

Dirtbag and Faux had once dated and although their relationship
was over, it took him months and a restraining order before he could
let go. Her pool was not well maintained and the water was heavily
chlorinated to address the filth from all the kids, so I always hesitated
to swim and never stayed in the water for very long. When we arrived,
my friend Brown was already there, courting Faux in earnest now that
she was no longer tied to Dirtbag. I didn't see what her suitors saw in
her, but they were legion.

We went inside and changed and Brody slipped down into the
water and hung along the pool's edge. Against the white sheet of his
upper arm, his self-given tattoo of a cross appeared crude and black as
if it had been carved by a heated knife. Bay waded into the shallows
and stood a few feet away, sliding her hands atop the water. "What is
up with those two?" I asked J-Bird as she swam toward me in the deep
end. But the closer she came, the less I cared. She treaded water in
front of me and once or twice her inner thigh would brush the inside
of my thigh and it was thrilling.

"Could you save me if I were drowning?" she asked. Her back was
turned to what little light came in through the windows and her face
was a black void and therefore I could not be sure of her intentions.
All I had to go on was the brushing of her legs and her voice, itself a
brush stroke that was soft and tentative.

"Probably." I was careful to keep my face straight and match her voice so I would not reveal the pleasure of her company.

"Good," she said, sinking beneath the water. I looked for her below me, but I couldn't see beneath the surface. When she didn't come up right away, I put two and two together and submerged. I found her on the bottom of the pool on her knees. Her eyes were closed and I think she was smiling. I swam behind her and slid my hands under her armpits and swam her to the surface.

"You're pretty good," J-Bird said, clearing her eyes.

In a deadpan voice, I replied that I had learned to swim in the Atlantic Ocean. The Atlantic was so far from Utah that I wondered if I appeared exotic.

"That explains it," she said, obviously humoring me.

Bay and Brody had since climbed out of the pool and gotten dressed. They were sitting in chairs that were far apart. "Fuck this, let's go." Brody got up and walked outside.

"That's our cue," I said to no one in particular.

J-Bird and I dried off and dressed. We thanked Faux and I told Brown to remember that shit is also brown and I'd see him later. He gave me that look that said, *Dude, I know you don't think that what I'm doing is worth a shit, but I've got to try.* A couple days would pass and I would learn that when Brown left later that night, Dirtbag was waiting and stepped out of the shadows and cold-cocked him, breaking his jaw. A Jack-Mormon, Brown was Christ-like in his passivity and he forgave Dirtbag and they became friends. He must have known something I didn't because I never could understand how he could do that.

Brody was in the car smoking a cigarette and listening to loud music with the windows rolled up. He was angry and he made no attempt to hide the fact. Perhaps he thought he still had a chance of getting things right with Bay, but for whatever reason, he decided to drop me off first, which meant he would have to backtrack to get home. I didn't bother to point that out to him, though, because he wouldn't have listened to me, and because I was self-absorbed and didn't care. How could I possibly, given what was about to happen? Through no fault of my own, I had been chosen. That didn't happen very often, so when it did happen, manners be damned, I gave it all of my attention. Granted, had Brody turned to me and said, *Look, I know you've been chosen and everything, but if you don't help me right now, I may do something drastic*, I would have taken a deep breath, looked at him carefully, and asked *How drastic?*

Brody's Bug was well maintained and usually filled with racing grade, super high-octane gas. I'm not sure what difference it made in terms of speed, but psychologically that fuel was a game-changer and he rallied toward my house as if every tight turn and close call might undo his frustration and hatred for the night. J-Bird and I were amused by all the bouncing and sliding. One second we were on her side of the car, and the next she was forcing me against the glass of the passenger window, outside of which there could have been a house on fire and I wouldn't have noticed it. Bay sat silently in the front seat, and judging by the tightness of her face and her forward gaze, I knew Brody had no chance tonight or ever.

When we finally pulled up to my house, my heart was pounding and everything was so clear that I wondered if I even needed to ask J-Bird to come inside, or if she would just know to come with me because she, too, had been chosen. I climbed out of the back and J-Bird was already moving toward the open door, but she paused and her face opened into a question. *Why are you still standing there with that lump in your pants and that expectant look on your face? What? Did you think I had something for you?* My blood sank, and by God if it had run out of me and pooled, I would have drowned myself in it right then and there.

"It's early," she finally said, ending my delusion of paranoia. "Do you want to hang out?"

I said I did and that I would borrow my brother's car and take her home whenever she was ready. I had had my fill of Brody and Bay's drama, so I turned and walked toward my house without saying thanks or goodbye. Bay got out of the car and she and J-Bird whispered for a moment and then J-Bird floated down the driveway like a ghost and Bay and Brody drove away.

I didn't know the name of the day because it never mattered. The sun was up or down. My clothes were clean or dirty. I had a car or I didn't. My mother's room was far away upstairs, so my brother and I did and went and came as we pleased and most of the time she was none the wiser. Although it had been dark for several hours and each was like a layer of sleep, I put my finger to my lips as I opened the door and we walked inside and into my room. We stood there for a moment and looked at each other. We did not talk or turn on the light or play music. Instead, we undressed each other. As I rolled down J-Bird's panties and removed her socks, I heard scratching at the door. I opened it a crack and Sooner, our schnauzer-terrier mix, ambled in wagging his tail and sniffed J-Bird.

Once he decided everything was in order, he looked around the room and then turned around and went upstairs. I smiled as I listened to him climb the stairs one by one. As he had gotten older, he had gained a few pounds and preferred to spend most of his time with my mother. Back when we were kids, though, he was just as likely to pal around with us and get into mischief. My brother used to keep his stash in a little plastic film canister and when Sooner was about two years old he found it and ate the whole thing, which my brother put at around two grams. Sooner was wasted. He'd walk down the hall and we'd be nowhere near him and, in what was likely an act of canine paranoia, he would suddenly turn around as if he had been nipped on the ass.

Eventually we sat him upright on the couch in front of the TV and I swear he sat there motionless for over an hour. He might have blinked. Now it was eight years later and J-Bird and I listened to his nails tap as he walked down the hall toward my mother's room. The house returned to silence and J-Bird lay on the floor and her skin was so white and luminous I looked outside for the moon. My relationships with women typically went south soon after we screwed and I had zero reason to believe things would be different with J-Bird. But it didn't work out that way. That was the only night I spent with her, and for a while, at least, we remained friends and sometimes I honestly believe it might make a difference if I knew why.

★ ★ ★

Greer points to a mourning dove roosting in the old blue spruce. She says, "Dad, I want it to hold me."

★ ★ ★

We had been drinking since well before sundown and now it was two hours after and the puerile madness that slept a dull sleep had awakened. About twelve of us stood clutching beers around a small fire we had made not thirty yards from the end of the suburb below

Bell Canyon Reservoir. We dug a deep pit and rimmed it with stones so that it would not be seen nor carried away by the wind that would gust and die in the foothills each night and was days ahead of late spring storms. Dilson was there, as were Cleese, Reed, Brody, Tosser, Dirtbag, and a few younger kids, wannabes from school. A goddamn concoction.

Below us, through the dense scrub oak, we could see the road stretch away a quarter-mile to the west and then split north and south on Dimple Dale Road. The road south led to that spot where my friend Willie's little brother wrecked his car and it burst into flame. He tried to crawl out the back, but he didn't make it and in that ashen state he resembled someone overtaken by lava. To the north was the small corral where Charlie the cow lived and was being studied. Charlie was the first bovine to test an artificial heart, so we left him alone. Tosser's house was situated on the corner where the roads met. We would park our cars there so as to end our association with them and we would walk the old mining road to our fire pit in the foothills.

The police regularly patrolled the area, sometimes with their lights off, but from where we stood we could see cars approach from two miles out. They did not stand a chance of surprising us. But on that night the threat did not come from without; it came from within and there was chemical violence afoot. Right around the time the night peaked, a storm moved in from the southwest. First the wind and then rain and the light, icy snow known as *gropple* pelted the ground like bits of Styrofoam. Lone Peak loomed ten thousand feet above us and the lightening refracted and paled its granite face, illuminating the now super-heated clouds and the eyes of birds roosting in the blue branches. If sunlight warms and moonlight mystifies the human face, lightning shows what is murderous in each of us.

Reed had wandered off to take a piss and he sang some drunken song as he wobbled out there in the scrub oak and the sage-sweetened darkness. I do not know whose idea it was to leave the fire and hunt Reed, but the moment someone said, "Let's get that fucker," like a band of albino Masai warriors, the throng of boys guzzled their beers and spat the foam into the wind and looked about wildly for clubs or spears. After the first drunken oath was shouted from the fire, Reed was on the run. We could hear him crashing through the scrub oak and that would set us running like a pack of sloppy hounds.

I knew it was not safe to wander too far from the group, which at any moment might turn on me. But the mob was too noisy to have any chance of getting Reed. I let the belching throng get ahead of me and then I stole off into the scrub and sat listening. The small, worried chirps of a bird rose out of the scrub to the east. I turned my face south and listened. Something large was moving carefully through the scrub about twenty yards above me. I cupped my ears and listened some more. Silence. Then more movement. I considered alerting the throng to my find. "Not yet," I whispered. Getting close enough to put salt on his tail would almost be as good as clubbing him.

Years of dead leaves lay on the ground and they were soaked with rain. Once I was within ten yards or so of the area where I heard the movement, I went down on all fours and crawled below the scrub. The wind was blowing down from above me and as it moved over the Earth it made a low hum that was loud enough to cover the sound of my stalking. I was drunk, but the closer I got to pouncing on Reed and maybe clubbing him a couple times, the more my adrenaline surged and energized my blood.

The throng moved off to the west and back toward the fire, alternately cursing Reed and assuring him it was safe to come out. I wanted to yell out, *He's over here, you stupid fucks!* But I held my tongue and moved to within ten feet of my prize. As I slowly rose from hands and knees and prepared to leap over the brush and onto Reed, a bedded mule deer exploded from the scrub oak and bounded into the night. I couldn't see the deer, but I could hear it make its way up the side of the mountain and toward the reservoir. It would take that deer a few minutes to summit the ridge, but it went quiet long before that. I knew he was about thirty yards above me, listening to me breathe, maybe smelling me now that the wind had shifted. My human stink of sweat, booze, cigarettes, soap, and the sweet hair of meadow animals. Reed never did come back. He doubled round and snuck down to his car and drove away with his lights off.

I may have slept over at Tosser's two or three times in my life and never completely willingly. Usually I would miss my ride and either have to stay there or walk three miles through the dunes and farmland to get home. This wasn't a big deal when it was daytime and I was sober. But by the end of a night of drinking, I was tired and going home felt like defeat. The night we hunted Reed, Tosser's mom was out of town. This fact didn't change anything. Whether she was there or not did not affect how I felt.

But in every other case an absent parent meant less hassle, so it was by default that I agreed to stay that night. It was convenient to believe that Tosser's dead sister was somehow responsible for the cold, somber feeling of that house. Since the dead-dead are quickly removed from sight, I don't know the extent to which they inform our lives. But the *living* dead move about in silence and demand their share of space. They impinge.

Tosser and his mother's guilt, sadness, and anger became palpable realities. And I sensed them in the house's darkness as they floated in its stagnant air like toxic air biscuits. I viewed Tosser and his mother as effects rather than as the cause of the malaise, and thus I always expected to see his dead sister sitting on her bed doing girl stuff like combing her hair, looking at pictures, or playing with herself; or maybe I half-expected to feel her laying hands on me at night. Some part of the brain whips up ghosts, and hers haunted me. The alcohol left me in a weakened state, so I curled up on the couch with a single blanket and tried to fall asleep as quickly as I could.

By and by, the night went by and the clock tongues swung deep in the house. In a dream I am walking through a familiar cornfield ravaged by locusts. The sun is hot and bright and the brown stalks lay broken in the pounded dust. For a moment I am seduced by this warm place, this reprieve of the dream. Then I see an African boy lying face down between the furrows. I'm afraid, but I kneel and turn him over and he looks at me with demon eyes of emerald fog and lips swollen and cracked from thirst. I woke up and felt my heart thumping hard and crazy from the sight of that ruined boy. I was never so thankful for a sunrise and I opened the sliding door and stepped outside to have a cigarette. Above me on the hill, Tosser's dogs peered down at me from their kennel. I stood and smoked while my double walked up there, opened the cage, and watched them bolt into the dunes.

I was not from around there, but I knew the dunes as well as anyone because I had almost died in them. Brody, Tosser, Deeg, and I had sluffed school and gone to Brody's house high on the hill. While there, we raided his fridge and his parents' liquor cabinet. By the time Deeg and I started our walk home, I had eaten four pieces of chicken and drank a Molotov cocktail of whisky, beer, rum, and schnapps. It was a very cold and gray December day and I was grossly underdressed in my jeans, oxford shirt, cardigan sweater, and light shoes. I put a drumstick in my pocket and we said goodbye to Tosser as we passed his house on the corner and began our steep ascent into the dunes.

My shoes were useless in the icy snow and I was so drunk I could not stand up anyway. I crawled the last few feet on my hands and knees and when I reached the top I staggered to my feet and swayed drunkenly with a hand under each armpit. Deeg had already cut out across the snow-crusted sand. I stood there teetering and watched him get farther and farther away. Finally he stopped and yelled at me to catch up. When he turned just so, I could see the spikes of his Mohawk pierce the air.

I took a few steps and stopped. My body was under attack. My heart had worked furiously to get me up the hill, but in the process it had accelerated the spread of the heavy, poisoned blood throughout my body. I collapsed and vomited fire that melted a putrid hole in the ice and snow. Deeg came back and yelled at me to get up. Seeing I couldn't stand on my own, he tried to help me and I said ruthless shit to him and told him to leave me alone.

What happened after that is blurry and fragmented. Deeg left me in the snow and walked back to Tosser's, where apparently he called Curtis and told him about me. I don't know how long I had been out there in the snow by the time Curtis appeared on the northern horizon and then carried me out of the dunes. I also don't know what he was thinking by showing up on a scooter, which I had no hope of staying on in my condition. As he tried to get me on the scooter, Charlie the cow and several sheep watched us from their corral. I never thought I'd envy a cow, and certainly not Charlie with his iffy ticker, but that is exactly what I did as I staggered half-frozen there on the roadside.

The situation was dire because of my physical condition, of course, but Curtis must have also wondered when our luck was going to hit rock bottom and a police cruiser would come around the corner. A car did come as he struggled without success to coax me onto the back of the scooter. A couple of nice old ladies pulled up in a Lincoln Town Car and asked if I was okay. While Curtis was busy trying to craft a lie, I remember becoming acutely aware of how cold I was, and it was at that moment I opened the door of the car and fell into the back seat, which was covered in luxurious faux red velvet.

I realize that what happened next doesn't make any sense, but I swear those old ladies then drove off with me in the back seat. Had they not rounded the corner and seen Deeg sitting on the curb in front of Tosser's house, who knows where they would have taken me?

"Do you know this boy?" the driver asked.

Deeg walked over to the car, looked inside, and saw me sprawled on the seat.

"I hate to say it, but I do," he said.

When I awoke an hour later, I was at Dilson and Curtis's house, lying on the downstairs couch. A pile of blankets lay atop me and the air was hot and smelled of the pinion that burned in the stove. Dilson, Deeg, and Curtis were looking at me, waiting for me to regain consciousness. Curtis said I was lucky to be alive. Then I looked down and saw my father rubbing my frozen feet. I don't know if he was really there or if I dreamt him. Thanks just the same.

After I smoked my cigarette and quit my fantasy of springing Tosser's dogs, I went back inside and sat on the couch. A few minutes later, Tosser walked in wearing a towel and combing his ridiculous and sweet-smelling flop of hair. He agreed to drop me off on his way to work. When I got out of the car, what I saw of the world was wide awake and bustling and I wanted no part of it. The alcohol and cornfield encounter had sucked me dry, so I went straight to my room and went to bed. I had been asleep for I don't know how long when I heard my bedroom door hit the closet door behind it. I had learned to leave it open a crack for Sooner who, if the door was closed, would sit and scratch it until I let him in.

Sooner was like a warm, furry pig and I enjoyed his company, so I lay there waiting for him to jump up on my bed and nap with me. I opened my eyes and looked at the floral print on my sheets. I guessed it was somewhere around noon. I knew for sure that it was a beautiful spring day and I was going to spend it all lying in bed with a vicious hangover. A few seconds passed and still no Sooner. Well fed on table scraps, Sooner was several pounds overweight, and he could not jump up on the bed without preparation. To this end he sat on his haunches, wiggled an anticipatory wiggle, and then jumped onto my bed. But I did not hear the tags on his collar jingle; nor did I feel his considerable heft.

Despite the sensorial details to the contrary, I thought I was dreaming when the paralysis came. I had no reason to be afraid, so I decided to trust what I thought must be a waking dream. It was an innocent mistake: not far above my left ear, I heard a voice. Neither male nor female, it said, "I knew you would come back." I tried to rise, but I could not. Then I felt a putrid succubus lick my ear. We do not realize we are being followed by the body of our fears. Now this stranger wants my children, wants to watch them from a park bench beneath the trees in the distance.

★ ★ ★

I will keep them from you, demon.
I will etch their names
on the canine tableaux, and they will
gnash at you from the dark
shelter of my stone dead mouth.

PART FOUR

EARTHSHINE

AND SOMEWHERE IN ME TOO IS THE PATH DOWN TO THE CREEK
GLEAMING IN THE DARK, A WAY OUT OF THERE.
—SHARON OLDS

My older sister Nicole was the first to defy history and marry in the spring of her twenty-first year. She had left home right after graduating high school and moved to Idaho Falls to care for my grandmother, Iris. Fifteen years later I would learn that the primary reason she left was to get away from my mother, whose chronic depression had taken its toll. Despite being a straight "A" student and, at least early in her life, regularly attending church, Nicole could get into what for her was some pretty serious trouble.

I remember her coming home late one night sauced off her ass. I could hear her mumbling and clunking around upstairs as she lurched from one side of the house to the other. I thought she had gone to bed, but the next morning my mother found her asleep naked in

the bathtub. Her antics were among some of the most memorable
and notorious because they were few and far between; that is, compared with mine and my brother Christian's. Or at least that is how
it seemed.

Perhaps because she was a girl and the oldest, Nicole probably had
less opportunity to get into real trouble. And it didn't hurt that she
was a good student and hung around with a fairly straight-edge group
of girls. Regardless, what it all boiled down to was that Nicole was at
home more and therefore had much greater exposure to my mother's
bouts of depression. Many years later, in an act of self-admonition, my
mother would muse about how truly bad it must have been for Nicole
for her to go to Idaho Falls, which she said was like *going backwards*. It
was there that Nicole met her first husband, Ruglus.

Ruglus's family lived in Scottsdale, Arizona, and they were relatively well-to-do. Of course the *idea* of their wealth did not matter,
but when my mother learned the wedding would take place at the
groom's country club in Scottsdale, the body of things changed from
a harmless idea into a masked child holding a big, bloody knife in its
bedeviled hand; if only because my mother and father, who had separated long ago, were not in a position to pay for such extravagance.
Had the groom's parents been more refined and spoken a few reassur-
ing words, the affair might have been enjoyable, especially for my sister, who I know struggled with her own doubt as well as my mother's
assessment of the groom as a condescending son of a bitch.

Turns out he was, but at that age who wants to see the future as
doomed? In that environment of mistrust, saguaro, hurt feelings, oco-
tillo, and hostility, each weak thing was swept up in that dust devil of
shit and desert funkiness and there was nothing anyone could do to
change it. For gatherings like that, there was only one philosophy:

Drink and be merry, for tomorrow I will be at the bottom of some shit heap with a hangover, and beautiful, hateful, and powerful people will be standing atop it, yelling profanities and hurling turds down at me. If I were not nearing the peak of my power at the time of the wedding, I might have suffered.

I had flown down early to sunbathe and explore the desert. These days when I fly it takes days of mental preparation and a tranquilizer to board a plane. And there are perfectly good reasons for that, although none of them is rational except for my underlying fear of being in an enclosed space and falling thirty thousand feet to the Earth. But in 1987 the only plane wreck any one ever heard about was the one in the Andes because the survivors had eaten their friends. My mother and father flew down early, too, and the night before the wedding the three of us drove to the airport and picked up Christian.

We drove north toward the hotel where we were staying. Christian was unusually animated and talkative. I was feeling pretty good myself. My mother was driving and my father sat next to her and commented on how, with the exception of the heavy odor of orange blossoms, this was not the Phoenix he remembered from his college days. But really everything seemed fine and I was happy to be there. In an attempt to share my satisfaction, I looked over at my brother. "What the hell is all over your glasses?" I asked, perhaps a bit too loudly. Christian tried to shush me with his lips, but it was too late: My mother was already looking at him in the rearview mirror and my father had turned around and now everyone saw the vomit dripping from Christian's face and glasses. Apparently he had tried to barf out the window and the desert wind blew it back in his face.

That is Arizona: a place that takes whatever you give it, magnifies it, and then returns it to you. Therefore, don't go to Arizona if you are drunk and need to vomit, are unenlightened, or if you think the desert is a barren wasteland with no value other than what value developers give it.

"Oh, Jesus Christ!" my father said, shaking his head in frustration and disgust.

"What did you do?" my mother barked angrily. "Are you drunk?"

Christian removed his glasses and asked if anyone had a tissue. Then, with a sheepish grin he said, "No, I'm not drunk," as if there had never been a more absurd question in the entire history of the world.

"Don't you lie to me!" my mother scolded.

My brother couldn't get the grin off his face, which is probably why he finally confessed he had had too much whiskey on the plane.

"You think?" I asked, enjoying the comedy of the moment.

But then Christian looked at me and my smile drooped: I realized I had let him down by alerting my parents to his intoxication. "Sorry," I whispered. But he didn't respond. Instead he shut his eyes and wished away the drunken moon.

When my sister said I was at her wedding, I told her I'd have to take her word for it. But I do recall the reception at the country club and how strange it was to mingle with my mother's side of the family. Most of them came off as staunch Mormons and had come down from Utah and Idaho to attend the celebration, which included freshly pre-pared gourmet food and a large cooler of ice-cold beer. I wasted no time getting wasted.

I got to hand it to my Mormon cousins, though: they were experts in wholesome entertainment. So genuine was their mirth, I remember taking a couple of them aside and, under my breath, asking if they had been drinking. *Heck no, cousin!* they would say, their cheeks flushed from dancing. That is part of the deception, isn't it? I could be the only person drinking in a room full of sober people, and by night's end I could convince myself they were all drunk. Fortunately, so long as my brother, sister, and her friends were there, I didn't have to drink alone.

Nor did I have to piss alone: Standing at the urinal next to me was the Chef, a white-haired man in his forties who blushed when I complimented his food. We made small talk while we peed and then I told him to take it easy, zipped up, and headed out. The reception lasted for about three hours and we all got back to the hotel somewhere around 10:00 p.m. In those days I didn't wear any underwear and I hadn't brought a bathing suit, so when my brother and a few of my sister's friends decided to go hot tubing, I either had to go in the buff, wear a pair of my mother's underwear, or not go. "What the hell," I said, holding up a pair of scarlet underwear. I never thought I would wish I had some Speedos, but there I was, wishing I had some Speedos. My father looked at me and laughed.

"You're not going to wear those, are you?"

I was in pretty good shape, plus I was pie-eyed drunk, so I said, "Sure, why not?"

Christian and I were the first to get in the hot tub, which was fine with me because I was feeling a tad self-conscious in my mother's underwear. Once my sister's friends—a dude and a couple of girls— joined us a few minutes later, Christian produced a "pinner" from his shirt pocket and fired it. Sometimes he'd get stuck with Iowan dirt weed or some other shit that would work lightly for about thirty minutes before turning into a splitting headache. But that night he had some Columbian "kind," courtesy of my father, who had recently made the acquisition while visiting his old friends Gordon and Bobby in New York. In fact, whenever my father visited us from back east, the first chance I got I would rifle through his suitcase in search of his New York produce. The kids on my block—Mormon and non-Mormon alike—were more than happy to partake of these beautiful brown buds.

By the time the joint had gone around the hot tub twice, both it and I were gone, blown into the night and stars that hung above the desert I could not see but knew was out there somewhere. My sister had a couple of attractive friends, but the two I sat between in the hot tub did not appear desirable even through the sexed-up and indiscriminate lenses of my beer goggles. In fairness to them, as the saying goes, I was too drunk to fuck and my organ was dead on arrival in that vat of heat. Moreover, while I could get away with drinking a couple beers after I had gotten high, doing the opposite was like asking for face-time with the porcelain god. I had ignored the age-old wisdom and now I was going to pay.

I did a quick internal scan of my body and wondered if I still had a chance to reverse course. In my life I have been fortunate enough to have had a few conversations of true consequence and the conversation in the hot tub was not one of them. But there was a lot of laughter and during a fit of it I discreetly exited the tub, put my hands in front of my package, and walked quickly over to the swimming pool.

I dove in and, short on breath, swam not very far underwater. The water was cool and light on my skin, and when I opened my eyes they were clear and did not burn. I surfaced, took a deep breath, and this time dove straight down. With nobody as my witness, I stayed down long enough to glimpse thirty cents on the bottom of the pool and retrieve a nickel of it before returning to the surface and placing the coin on the pool's edge. As a kid I was pliant enough to swim like Aqua Man by placing my hands at my side and using my body's momentum to undulate porpoise-like through the water. It had been a while, but I rediscovered that old style and swam a few feet like that. I found myself in the deep end with plenty of room, and I proceeded to twirl and tumble in what was my first performance of water ballet.

Out of the water, I would not dare attempt a backflip, and I had dared only once to try a front flip on a trampoline when I was thirteen years old. I flipped alright, but I landed wrong and my right knee smashed my face and broke everything except the bone. Under water, I was fearless. Not only did I do front and backflips, I did twists and log rolls and walked on my hands before falling over in slow motion. I felt an amazing sense of control and rightness, as if at any moment I would discover I could breathe underwater, at which point I would climb out of the pool, say my goodbyes, and hop the next bus to the ocean.

But of course my belief was not so great, and I was not so high, that I would risk breathing under the water. Instead I would kick slowly to the surface, where I would expose only my mouth and nose holes. Then I would suck the cool night air that was complicated by the heavy fragrance of orange blossoms, and whose necessity made breathing intensely pleasurable.

I had just finished a complex routine with which the judges would be pleased. Then I made my third ascent to the surface. Once there, I pushed back my hair and saw a man sitting on one of lounge chairs, watching me. It was the Chef, and he was still wearing his white Chef shirt. *What the fuck is he doing here?* I wondered. But I wasn't born yesterday. I glanced over at the hot tub, but I could not see anyone through the steam. Then I remembered my mother's underwear. Seeing me in those panties, would he be right to get the wrong idea? I had a choice to make: either stay where I was and remain in full display, or do just the opposite of what I wanted to do and swim *toward* the Chef and hide behind the poolside. I didn't want to be rude, so I decided to swim over and see what he wanted.

As I neared the pool's edge, the Chef sat up, walked over to me, and squatted.

"What's going on, man?" I asked, guardedly and with masculine bravado.

The Chef looked around and then at me.

"I thought maybe you'd like to go get high and hang out."

Luckily for me, I had already smoked and just gotten everything under control. Although there were other reasons, that was the only one I needed to decline his invitation.

"No thanks, man. I'm already kissed." Maybe not the best choice of words, or maybe the perfect choice of words, but just so there was no confusion, I added that I was already fucked up and then I returned to the middle of the pool. The Chef lingered for a couple of really long, awkward minutes. Then he got up and walked away.

Free from their burden, cats and dogs are frisky right after they shit; they run around in the grass and dart this way that way. That is sort of how I felt now that I was free of the Chef's erotic gaze. So it was with renewed vigor that I returned to my underwater world and attempted three consecutive backflips. Despite not having any formal training, things were going beautifully. My back was arched and I felt like a golden ring. I could feel the muscles in my neck as I went around once, then twice. In the process of spinning, I became disoriented, and on the third rotation I smacked my head on the bottom of the pool. A hail of stars blinked everywhere I looked. I worried I had a concussion.

I kicked toward the surface and climbed out of the pool. My brother and sister's friends were not in the hot tub. "Fuck," I whispered. The only choice I had was to return to the hotel room, which was across the parking lot. The night was chill and I didn't have a towel, so I folded my hands across my package and tried to keep a low profile. Fortunately, I didn't encounter anyone on my way to the room, but the door was locked and I had to stand out there under the light while my mother got out of bed to let me inside.

I pushed my way in and told my mother that I had hit my head. The room had two beds and my father acted like he was asleep in one of them.

"What do you mean you hit your head?" my mother asked.

"I mean I hit my head." I know she was just worried, but her questions were annoying and preventing me from lying down and going to sleep.

"Where did you hit it?"

Obviously there were at least two different answers to the question, depending on what she meant by *where*. Did she mean *where on my head* or *where at the hotel*? But that was exactly the kind of guesswork I wanted to avoid.

"Look, mom, if you don't stop talking, I'm going to get sick. Now please be quiet."

By then I had made it into the bed and under the sheet, where I shivered and eventually placed one foot on the floor to stop the spinning. My mother was hell-bent on keeping me awake so she could make sure I didn't have a concussion.

Making an appointment with the porcelain god is like making an appointment with the dentist when you've got a cavity: one can only avoid it for so long. Then my mother asked what I was doing before I hit my head, and it was as if she had breached a levy. "Fuck, I told you not to talk. Now I'm going to get sick." For the next two hours,

I knelt in front of the Porcelain God and saw my shadowy reflection in the toilet water. Disgusted with myself, I rested my head on the altar and spewed acid prayers and curses. And I swore oaths I hoped no one would hear, and I made promises my foolish self would not dream of keeping.

★ ★ ★

A couple years later, I met Kim in December of my nineteenth year, which was the lowest point of my life. The September before, I had rolled my Land Cruiser in Corner Canyon, not far from the place where J-Bird and I had sat three years earlier and looked across the valley and seen the horses with their heads to the barn and, farther out, the state prison all lit up like an empty carnival of watchtowers and electrified concertina wire. My physical injuries were comparatively minor, but I was filled with guilt and anger and painkillers. I had also become a cocaine zombie, my pockets empty and my nose bleeding as I mindlessly roamed the Salt Lake Valley, wandering from party to party, from shadow to shadow, looking for something or someone to save me from my self-made hell. Had I not been poor, I might have gone on like that, but I was poor, so there was no future in my habit unless I was willing to steal. I wasn't willing. Thus I had almost reached the end of the line of cocaine when I met Kim, a taciturn, wholesome, Westside girl from a blue-collar family.

When I see pictures of us from those early years, I cannot quite believe those two kids are Kim and me. I am estranged from our images because we look so new and I can't remember how I looked at the world then. But it is easy to see what I saw in Kim, that barefoot and sun-browned teenager walking taut and awake through the desert and along the red shore of Lake Powell. If I had no memory of those early days, this moment might remain buoyant or appear to rise a little. But the past is the gravity of the present moment. It pulls us back to the Earth, to where everything that matters starts and ends. In this calamitous present, I will try to remember what I loved. I will start with the reddish-peach color of Kim's skin after two days in the desert, how it resembled the stone and the sand and the sun behind the clouds. Yesterday we took Wilder and Greer to the river and we spent as much time planning and preparing for the outing as we did on the outing itself. It used to be we could decide to go to the lake, pack the car, and be on the road within an hour.

The last time we went to Powell we arrived after dark and made camp in the headlights. I had borrowed a tent from my friend Dilson and it was complicated enough to where, instead of popping it, I spread it across the stones and the small life. Then we laid our sleeping bags atop the tent and watched the stars, which in the darkness of that place are entire. Deeg was with us on that trip, and later that night when Kim and I made love, I could hear him mocking me from his sleeping bag, which he had laid in the dirt a few yards away. In all the years that I had known him, Deeg had not learned to drive; nor did he ever have a girlfriend. These were the basic building blocks, and without them Deeg had become a kind of oddity or court jester and for him there was pleasure and power in that role. Whatever he was, though, I would rather be me.

Once we had made it through courtship, Kim and I entered the physical stage of our relationship. Of course having *any* sex at that age was desirable personally and socially. But having it three or four times a week was like money in the bank. I was lean with it. Contrary to the prevailing attitude toward premarital sex, deep down—perhaps even below consciousness—every boy I knew understood that having sex, regardless of what it meant, was *the* underlying reason for having a girlfriend. After we exit this stage and become adults, we project backward on our childhood and decide things ought to be done differently. Most adults with children are necessarily and maybe even justifiably hypocrites.

I see myself at forty walking up on me and Kim when I was twenty and she was eighteen and we were going at it under one of the darkest skies in the Northern Hemisphere. *Excuse me*, I would say, squatting a couple a feet away. My twenty-year-old self would be annoyed but unafraid, and despite her disbelief, Kim would recognize me instantly. After everyone had settled down and my twenty-year-old counterpart had hid his boner, I would continue: *What I am about to tell you has nothing to do with sin.* That would get my attention because everyone knows sin is the torch-lit path to hell. *This is what we know: Should you become pregnant, you are asking for difficulty of the profoundest, most far-reaching kind.*

At exactly that moment, a meteor would enter Earth's atmosphere and rip a fiery canyon into the blackness, punctuating my point. *You two are nowhere near being emotionally, psychologically, and financially ready to have a child. That is especially true for you, young man. Do you even have a job?* I would leave it at that. Then I would press a couple hundred bucks into my twenty-year-old hand, suggest I read *The Origin of Species* "yesterday," and, when the time came, invest in Google.

The next morning we made a small fire and Deeg wondered if I weren't part black-tail jackrabbit. As I got older, most of my sexual pleasure came from giving Kim pleasure, but that wasn't my approach as a teenager. I was putting my key in the lock and that was all that mattered. Thus Deeg's teasing and mocking did nothing except underscore how his default position was celibacy. I finally said, *Yeah, well, keep talking. Keep shitting the bed.* Then I opened a couple cans of beans and placed them in the coals. The sun had just risen and it sat on the horizon like an unblinking eye. We ate the beans and Deeg and I squatted near the fire. A user of neither nicotine nor caffeine, Kim was ready for the day the moment she woke up. But that was not the case with me and Deeg. I cracked a coke and drank it between drags on my cigarette. Deeg did the same and afterward loaded a pipe and toked.

"Breakfast of champions, aye Deeg?"

Deeg grinned and handed me the pipe.

"Hippie speedball. Here, medicate," he said, in that strange, pressurized voice of someone holding his hit.

Before I accepted it, I looked at Kim and she rolled her eyes. Back then I was annoyed by her disapproval, but I was fortunate to have met someone for whom chemicals had almost no appeal. Kim was the opposite of my first serious girlfriend, the Egyptian (the master eye-roller): she was stable, grounded, didn't use drugs, drank very little alcohol, and was a virgin. In this town, one would assume she was Mormon. But she was a-religious. "I'll just take a small hit," I told her as she stood, brushed the sand from her lovely ass, and walked down to the lake. Deeg and I straightened up camp and then I took our spoons and the empty bean cans and followed Kim.

She had since taken a seat and was holding her knees on a slab of sandstone jutting out over the water. I scrambled down and dipped the cans into the water and then rinsed the spoons. I looked up at Kim and noticed her bathing suit gathered between her legs. I had just been there a few hours before, but I never tired of imagining my next visit. Kim caught me looking at her and turned away her body. "I'm going to douse the fire and we're going to go for a walk before it gets too hot."

I placed the cans on top of the ledge and climbed up to them. "Why don't you come along? Then we'll go swim."

Deeg and I ran, leapt, and frolicked like mindless, desert imps. We played follow the leader and climbed giant sandstone boulders that had shorn off cliffs rising into the hard blue sky a quarter-mile away. It was still early and Kim wasn't high, so instead of joining us, she walked along and studied the ground, stopping occasionally to pick up a rock or the shell of some long-dead invertebrate. At twenty, I was still caught between nurturing my relationship with Kim and spending time with my friends. But when buds were involved, the scale tipped in favor of my friends, with whom I would enter the haunted world. It would be another hour or two before we could comfortably swim, so I walked down to the lake and tried to sweet-talk Kim into walking up a little side canyon on a lizard-hunting expedition with me and Deeg.

As luck for the lizards would have it, in our overzealous if not outright compromised state, we had overlooked a central fact: lizards are cold blooded and would not appear until the sun had climbed well into the sky. After it became clear that there would be no hunting, Deeg said he was going to *piss off back to camp*. That was his British way of informing me of his plans to go and smoke more drugs. When it came to smoking pot, Deeg could never stay high enough, long enough, so he would have to smoke more grass, more often.

I wasn't great at holding down a job, but Deeg had mastered unemployment. He might work long enough to get his first check, which he would then use to buy the biggest bag of dope he could find. Then he would run away with it. Of course, at the rate he consumed, his purchase would not last for long. Eventually, Deeg quit work altogether because he found that he could leech off my brother, who was also a heavy smoker and in his mind had elevated smoking to an art form.

I didn't find pot all that interesting as a subject of study, but I did enjoy smoking it and lying in the sun, shooting hoops, or later reading Percy Shelley, Keats, Rilke, and Whitman under its influence. I preferred reading poems to prose because it was easier to concentrate on and remember the shorter lines, although I do recall making some breakthroughs while reading Emerson. I guess I was a bit of a leech myself because I can count on one hand the times I bought grass. There may have been other times, but I don't remember them. Without my own stash, I was an infrequent visitor to my brother's apartment downtown, which, at the peak of his drug days, was something of an art studio inside an armpit inside a litter box.

My brother lived there with his friend Sumo, who not only tolerated his cats Squawker, Smiley, Cujo, and Schmiggler, but also Deeg, who had inserted himself into my brother's bedroom and seldom left it. For whatever sadistic reason, Deeg saw it as his duty to bathe the cats, which he usually did once my brother had left for work. Cats often appear in my brother's artwork, so it is possible Deeg was preparing them to be painted, although that seems unlikely since the cats in the paintings bear little resemblance to their living inspiration. For instance, one cat was depicted as bipedal and waving the hang-loose sign.

Who can say how many baths those cats had seen since Deeg arrived. They would have seen many more were it not for the heroics of Schmiggler, a bushy Persian that shrank to the size of a golden rat when wet. Deeg had bathed the other three cats and now it was Schmiggler's turn. But because of past experience, Schmiggler decided she wasn't going to step paw into that water. When Deeg tried to force the issue, she bit him on the shoulder, leapt from his arms, ran out of the room, and jumped off the second-story balcony, landing in a juniper bush below. This incident became known as City Schmiggler's revenge.

Three humans and four felines cohabitating in such a small space did not lend itself to cleanliness. I know because there were two litter boxes and for a while there the cats had to use their own shit for litter. But no one seemed to mind the filth, least of all Deeg, who would go days without taking a shower. In the wide open desert, cleanliness did not matter so much, and Deeg was always an eager and willing travel companion provided, of course, there was grass.

Kim and I watched as Deeg disappeared over the ridge. Lizards or no lizards, the canyon looked promising and we followed it until we came to a cave formed by an overhang, where it appeared many animals had sought shelter from the sun. The delicate tracks of birds etched the red sand and tiny craters marked the places where the birds had pecked at seeds or hapless bugs or had tweezed a blade of dry grass for the nest. There were larger tracks, too. Wind had not gotten to one fresh set that led to the back of the cave where a rabbit had been eaten. Sand and blood gobs lay scattered among bone bits, dried viscera, and rags of hide. Were I versed in superstition, I would have sat and augured their meaning. The predator's belly hair cleft the dirt and I imagined a coyote pinning the jack with its paws and looking from side to side as if at any moment the prize might be taken from him.

Kim joined me and we looked down at the yellowed skin and saw how the hair parted in the breeze. "Smells sour," Kim said, hiking her nose. Her bikini top had slipped down, revealing a stripe of white skin and the pale-pink crest of her right areola. Further influenced by the grass and the sun, I convinced Kim to accept me in the dirt. I took off my shirt and spread it across the sand. Once she was seated on my shirt, I kneeled between her legs and lowered her by the arms until she was supine. I rested on my forearms and kissed her deeply as the ants excavated marrow from the hollow of a bone. I then reached down and rubbed the silky fabric and I could feel the hot features beneath it. Patience has never been my strong point, and when I slipped my hand beneath her suit, she stopped me on the threshold. "Not yet," she said in a hard whisper.

She placed my hand atop her and when she was ready she slipped her suit to one side, took me between her thumb and finger, and guided me in. I had off her top and I could not keep my mouth from the cool flesh and I went back and forth from nipple to nipple as if trying to decide the better flavor of ice cream. She tasted of sun, sweat, baby oil, saliva, wood smoke, and earth so faint it was more like breath than dust. She tasted elemental. If the timing were right, Kim would pull me and hold me inside, but this was not one of those times. Sensing I was about to peak, she kissed my ear and whispered, "You can't do that inside." She was sweet about it and the words were the final stroke and I pulled out and thrust hard and down between her legs as if I were inseminating the planet.

★ ★ ★

Wilder was about three when he first noticed Greer's anatomical differences. He pointed and laughed and said she had two bums.

★ ★ ★

My warm engine, wanting is what drives me. It is blue fire swirling inside a sheath of ice. But the Earth pulls at the material, at the bones and the skin and the blood. Life abides as its forms disperse. I've started my walk down the long road. At some point I too will step out of my body. I have dreamed of my eviction. The wolf spider will know what to do, will be the one to watch me go. The warm spring wind will blow my hair across the cemetery lawn and my old friends the crows will use it to pad their nests. By then my own parents will have become an ineffable calculus. I may have to stand on a chair and shield my eyes from the hard sun, but I can still see the place where I leave the road and it is not pretty. And what is art if not a momentary beautification of death?

I have no illusions. I use but am not lulled by metaphors. My death is real and it is going to happen, and then as now I will be afraid to let go.

I'm trying to see up ahead, but the road turns and falls. When I finally get wherever I am going, no one will be waiting. Not my dogs and cats; nor the members of my family; nor the people I wronged, which is good. I will have watched the body weather and erode; noted its terrible frailty; and witnessed the morphology of teeth that will not burn. What can I do in the meantime except redirect desire? The past may be gone or dissolving, but it is still more present than the future. I am trying to remember the beauty of the past. It is here, under a new definition.

★ ★ ★

The more I love, the more I fear death.

★ ★ ★

I was afraid the acid would turn loose some truer version of me or send me to a place from which I could not return. Without the gentle words of support from my brother, I would not have had the courage to drop. We were living at the house on Kramer Drive, the same house where everything had happened, and where it was rare to be alone. At any given time, three or four cars would be parked outside; people would be smoking on the deck; and music would drift out of the windows on warm days and nights. The first time I dropped, about ten of us were in my brother's room and I was chain-smoking cigarettes.

"Why do you have these?" I asked, holding up one of four pieces of rope that coiled under each corner of his bed.

My brother smirked.

"I use those to restrain Sex Kitten." SK was his long-time girlfriend whom he later discovered was sleeping with his friends, at least one of whom was standing next to him at that very moment. When used to describe the sexual activity of eighteen-year-olds, *sleeping* is a profound misnomer. My brother held out his open hand and confetti of acid lay in the center of it. I pressed the paper with the tip of my finger and held it in front of me, studying it as if it were a strange, new insect. Black pyramid.

"What's going to happen? Am I going to trip over my own balls?" I asked.

My brother and his friends laughed and messed my hair and slapped me on the back.

"The saying is 'tripping balls,' little brother. So no, man. You're not going to trip over your balls or anything else. You're going to awaken."

"That's good to know," I said, and then I placed the triangle of paper on the back of my tongue, which was a mistake because then I could taste the chemical bitterness.

My South Korean friend Doc was there, giggling, as were Tosser, Dirtbag, Cleese, and a few of my brother's friends. They took turns eating from my brother's hand. My father was staying with us while he tried to find a job in Salt Lake and he didn't get out of his flannel pajamas for three months. Many years later he would tell me how his decision to leave Maine and come to Utah to search for a job was one of the worst decisions he had ever made. But then he backtracked when he realized that if he hadn't come to Utah, he wouldn't have found a job in Idaho, met his second wife, and had my half-sister, Anna. After our conversation, I think we both realized that a man can in fact face north and south at the same time. I can't remember what he was doing the night I dropped acid, but my guess is not much because he was still in his pajamas when he loaned me his car. We made it all the way downtown to Gravity Hill before the acid kicked in and we started frying.

I parked on the hill beneath a naked maple and we got out and stepped into the knee-deep snow of late December. In the absence of sensorial discrimination, I had become deemphasized and tended toward inertia. Because everything was happening in my head and body, I didn't feel the need to move. I can't explain except to say my blood was flying like birds in a house with all its windows swung open. Then someone who was not really there said, *You are so lost*, and I laughed so hard I broke a blood vessel in my eye.

Doc walked over to where I was doubled over and he put his hand on my back. "You okay there, Boss?" he laughed. I was out of my right mind and I still felt weird when he called me that. He might have drank a split of the cheap champagne his parents always brought back and stockpiled after their frequent gambling trips to Wendover, Nevada, but he hadn't dropped or smoked so far as I knew. I was high as all get out, so I spoke to him as if he, too, were soaring. I asked him if he could hear the snow breathing and he said, "Oh boy, oh boy, oh boy." We had wanted to make a fire in the scrub below Gravity Hill, but we did little more than kick away the snow until the ground lay open. Meditation Chapel and memorials to the war dead squatted in the bare trees beyond the shrunken creek whose edges were silver with ice.

Whether the scene rebutted or proved the existence of the soul was impossible to say, but there was not a boy among us who would deny the entire Salt Lake Valley was populated by pilgrim and native ghosts alike and vendors of the end of days. For a time, and perhaps in an effort to decipher her dead daughter's whereabouts, Tosser's mom had done tarot, although she would neither confirm nor deny claims that the world was in fact ending. On such occasions, local radio stations broadcast the news that a meteor would collide with the Earth at a certain hour, or that such-and-such inexplicable calamity was upon us, and the hardware store down the street would host an end-of-the-world party and string balloons across the parking lot, play music, and offer hot dogs, sodas, and deep, end-of-the-world discounts.

I could not tell what Tosser thought about his sister's death or his mother's transcendent preoccupations because he never said anything about them. I could see where he had broken trail and had walked out across the common area and I followed in his tracks. Doc was close behind and I could hear him blowing into his hands. We stopped at the bottom of the hill so he could light a cigarette and then we caught up with Tosser at the chapel.

The doors were locked and Tosser shook them and the heavy chain made its noise. Doc stood on the steps and tried to blow smoke rings. Nothing held in the cold air.

"Give me a hand," Tosser said, standing below the chapel window, which was more like a thin turret cut out of the stone. I put my back against the cold wall and then he stepped into my hands and I lifted.

After a moment, I asked, "What do you see?"

"Let me down," he said, and so I did and his face looked gray.

"What is in there?" I asked again, amused by and afraid of his apparent reluctance to say. He lit a clove cigarette and it crackled when he drew from it.

"Take a look," he said, leaning against the wall and lacing together his hands. Tosser said to mind his cigarette and hoisted me up. "Do you see them?"

Most of the room was blocked from sight, but what I saw of the floor was white and strewn with small, dead birds that had flown in and had not found a way out.

We took State Street home. Doc drove because I had not come down far enough and Tosser promised that if we were to look at his head at that very moment, we would surely see it glowing like a star. I had known him for years and, other than what he had drawn in high school art class, that was one of the rare times he showed any imagination. I suggested he do acid more often and he laughed and said, "No fucking way."

State Street was strung with lights for the holiday season and I was a kid again watching fireworks ignite the water at Blue Hill. When we got to Doc's house, the next day had just begun. "Can you make it from here?" he asked. I said I could and he got out and left the door open and the car running. Tosser didn't want to go home and that was fine with me because I felt like I was driving a hovercraft and we hadn't even moved yet. I checked all the instruments and mirrors as if I were taking the driving test for my license. Then I backed out and off we went up 9800 South, a dark stretch of road flanked by desert on one side and the suburb on the other.

Maybe teenagers don't have as many lives as cats, but I lost at least one on that very road. I was with Doc and we had sat on our skateboards and lain back and were flying down the hill. Doc was somewhere out in front of me, but I couldn't see him or anything in the pitch and the sound of the wheels on the road made it impossible to hear anything except my own laughter. My eyes were watering in the cold night and I realized the limits of my vision when suddenly a man on an unlit motorcycle was in front of me and he turned just before we collided. As I've gotten older, I don't think I've run out of chances so much as I've stopped taking them.

I turned off the headlights and rolled up to the curb in front of my house. I made up a bed for Tosser on the downstairs couch and then climbed into my bed. My door was open and I could hear him carrying on about all the lights and shapes he saw when he closed his eyes. The longer he talked, the more agitated he became, until finally he asked me to talk him down. I saw the chapel and one of the birds I had seen tried to coax me in by feigning a broken wing. I was tempted, but I resisted the invitation and instead talked to Tosser until he was finally able to bed down on his own.

The summer before, I stood across from Doc and his father and sisters at his mother's open grave. Doc wore a curious black suit and his hair had just been cut and I could see where the barber had cut him too close above the ears and given him whitewalls. I had not seen Doc cry and I was touched and confused by how childlike he looked. Although I understood what was happening, and that no one would ever see Doc's mom again, it was not until I pondered Doc's suit that I felt any pain. For one thing, it looked tight and the pants might have been a tad short. The point is he looked like exactly what he was: a child burying his mother.

And his father? Turns out he could have said *Let's get this over with* and laid in the box with her that day and he would not have been too early. He took Doc and me to dinner a year or so before his death and I remember thinking then that he was the saddest man I'd ever met. But I really didn't understand what I was seeing: It wasn't so much that he was sad, it was that he was finished with life, long before it was finished with him. Doc understood this. Now I, too, know Doc's father had been dead since the death of his wife. When my back was turned, a graveyard crow flew overhead and dropped one of its feathers into the grave and that feather was him. There are many lights in the house of the body. Sometimes it takes years to turn them off. Sometimes days or hours.

Doc later joined the Marines and I guessed he did so out of desperation, but I could have been wrong. A year into his tour of duty he came home on leave and we went for a drive up Little Cottonwood Canyon. It was fall and I could smell the frost on the leaves when the wind shifted and blew into the car. As we drove past the fields that rivaled the monotony of the suburbs, and that still showed what this part of the world really looked like, he told me he didn't think he could do it anymore. He always wore his uniform and I remember the thick creases in his pants and shirt, how they lined up with the edges of his crew cut. For all but a few moments in my life at that time, I was the star in my own major motion picture. I was busy casting the show and delivering my lines. But my lines often depended on other people's lines. I was a quick study, though, so I asked Doc if there were any way he could get out.

"Not honorably," he said.

I thought he had opened the door a crack, so I pressed him: "So get out dishonorably."

Doc shifted in his seat and tapped the ash from his cigarette.

"That would not be a good idea, Boss."

We passed beneath the Mormon Perpetual Storage Vault and then the Gate Buttress, whose sheer granite face gleamed in the moonless night.

"You need to do for you, Doc."

He smashed his cigarette and looked at me for a couple of seconds and then back at the road.

"I *am* doing for me. You don't understand how it works."

Maybe I did, maybe I didn't. If there were a reason why he didn't think I understood commitment, I knew what it was. We know where we went wrong with people.

Before he left for boot camp, Doc and I had driven up to a place just off Dimple Dale Road known as The Beach. Some kids from school had built a fire and were drinking beers and smoking shit and Doc was the man of the hour because he was giving up the life and joining the Marines. I was dating Bay at the time, but she was grounded and so when the Egyptian and J-Bird showed up, they showed up without her. They stood on one side of the bonfire and I stood on the other and that distance seemed to work just fine. They were flanked by would-be suitors, but I knew the deal and so did the Egyptian.

Some of the boys were hair farmers, which is to say they had grown out their hair and we'd have to be blind or shut our eyes not to notice it wafting in the firelight. It was mountain hair whose sole purpose in life was to have cold wind blow through it. Swaddled in this rugged skull grass, their smooth, bright faces resembled those of lank, mannish women. Among these longhairs were the Schnazelkopf brothers, a pair of Jack Mormons, stag sons of God with a load in their pants and wood in their truck, which sank and bounced when they climbed in the back and pulled at the knotty limbs. When the pieces struck the dirt, they made the heavy sound of something that could hurt me.

They said the wood had been dead for a long time and would burn well. As if touching their hair would ruin it, whenever it curtained across their faces, like Cher they gyrated their upper bodies to remove it, only to have the long, thick shocks return an instant later.

According to plan, and like every other swinging dick, these boys stood downwind of the fire and close to J-Bird and the Egyptian. Now and then they would have to turn away from the immense heat and the sparks would go swirling by them like a species of biting moth whose life cycle was short and violent. The wind would die and each of them would turn back to the fire and their faces were sweating and flecked with mica dust.

The older Schnazelkopf brother eyed me warily, perhaps remembering the night he had gotten all hot for a drug skank and I had razzed him with a song whose lyrics were insulting at best. I must say I was wary of him as well, but only because he tried to strangle me. His face was calm now, as if it had been swept with the broom of everlasting peace. But put coke up that nose and beer in that stomach and his face would turn sallow and crazy like the sky before a freak dust storm.

Despite my relations with Bay and other girls in the interims, I struggled to stay away from the Egyptian. If Doc didn't know of my turmoil before that night at the Beach, he knew of it after. A time-lapse video recording would show people coming and going from the fire. They would return with ghosts on their arms; fidget with their noses; or crack a fresh beer while drawing from half-kissed cigarettes with their siren-red tips, all while gazing at the world through glassy eyes that would flicker beneath a film of blood-streaked water. And when out of that thick soup of fire, smoke, chemicals, and starlight rose the sweet possibility of lying with the Egyptian on the lee side of the wind-torn dune, it was as if Bay did not exist.

Doc appeared on the edge of the beach and he was backlit and blacked out by the climbing fire.

"I'm leaving, Boss. I'll wait for five, and then I'm going."

I knew he was disgusted with me for what I had not yet done. The Egyptian had been lying on her back. At the sound of Doc's voice, she peered up.

"Hi, Doc."

Doc raised a hand and said, "Hey," and then he turned and stepped below the horizon.

"Should we stay?" she asked.

I looked at the Egyptian and knew what awaited me: I looked at the night and did not. It was past midnight. We would have to walk the miles of pitch-black desert between us and home. I told her these things and lit a cigarette.

Then I heard Doc give up on me, get into his car, and drive away. A few minutes later, we saw his car far below us, its brake lights winking in the darkness. I thought maybe he would turn around and come back for us. Instead he turned on to Dimple Dale Road and soon was out of sight. I felt this terrible feeling rising up in my throat. Then I swallowed and it was gone.

The wind hadn't quit, but it seemed louder now as it dragged through the scrub oak and hissed across the sand. I took a swig of beer, rinsed, and spat it downwind. The tails of my open shirt whipped at the night. I was lord. We had a six-pack and ten cigarettes. The darkness was there for us. We would become stargazers and fitful sleepers after each silent conferral of tongues. I could smell the Egyptian's spit on my lips. We had six hours before sunrise. We would be making a sacrifice. Our longing might take minutes to kill.

★ ★ ★

I awoke to a fit of thunder as a storm moved over our house in Mill Creek. It was midnight in late May. I could hear the wind and hail striking and tearing the new leaves from the trees as the smell of ice poured in through the window. The floor and the room were so cold, I thought it could again be winter. I looked to see if Kim was awake, but it was too dark and then the lightning flashed across her sleeping face, which looked untroubled for the first time in months. The wind lifted the blinds and a small picture of us fell off the wall. But I stayed where I was because for once things were fine, I craved the storm, and the moment did not need changing.

In the morning I looked out Wilder's window to see how the robins in the apple tree had fared, but the nest was empty and the yard was littered with shingles, tree parts, and garbage from the cemetery. While everyone slept, I dressed and wolfed down a breakfast of toast and eggs. Then I slipped out into the yard to see all that the storm had done. I raked the leaves and branches into a pile together with the ribbons and balloons, one of which said *We miss you.*

As the day warmed, one by one Kim and the kids joined me outside. It was spring, after all, and we were through with waiting. Remnants of last night's storm, dark clouds turned over the eastern mountains while the western sky spread clear and blue. Greer was still tiny then and she would plop down and disappear behind the tomato plants. Now and then I'd see handfuls of dirt fly into the air and hear her sweet prattle and that is the reason I knew she was there.

Wilder turned a stone and found a sow bug killer crouched above her eggs. Excited and a little afraid, he stepped back and asked me what we should do and I said she meant us no harm and that we should leave her be. Kim wouldn't look at me, which is what she does when she's doubtful. She wanted it dead. I felt the frustration start in my chest and rise into my throat, but before it could turn into words and escape my mouth, I walked to the corner of the yard and started raking last year's dead leaves from beneath the pear tree.

My heart jumped at the sudden alarming calls of the robins, which had remained silent and hidden all morning. I turned and saw our cat Bella Jean leave the bushes and then slink low and fast toward the house as the frantic calls of the robins peaked behind her. Then I saw what they were so worried about: the chick they had been growing for the last few weeks hopped along the ground. Despite how the bird's head leaned to the side and its beak was pressed to its chest— the result, I guessed, of a deep bite to the neck—for a moment I let myself believe that the bird had gotten lucky and would be alright. Because I knew something about what it had taken to get it here, it was too hard to believe otherwise. But what I believe has nothing to do with the facts.

Kim walked over with Greer in her arms and Wilder at her side. "What happened?" she asked. The bird had hid itself behind some leaves and when I crouched down to spread them, the bird made a small chirp and blinked and we could see its heart beating in its chest. "Broken neck," I said, offering my best guess. My neighbor Arlene had also heard the commotion and came to the fence and looked over. "That's too bad," she said in that far off way that meant she'd seen this many times before. Wilder approached and looked at the bird and then looked at me and when I saw the confusion in his face I wanted to say, "Look, boy, do you see? This is what happens," so he would know and prepare for a life of it, but I also knew that the world would teach him just as it had taught me. I told Kim to take him and Greer inside.

Arlene had a BB gun she used to shoot rats several years back when the rats were plentiful and fat with rotting fruit. I asked her if she still had the gun even though I knew she still did, and she said yes and asked me if I wanted it even though she knew I did. Once Arlene had gone to get the gun, I knelt down by the broken bird and thought *I'm sorry* and *I should have protected you* and *I could kill that goddamn cat*, but I didn't say anything for obvious reasons.

A few minutes later Arlene returned with the gun and handed it over the fence. Once the gun was in my hands I said, "Fuck," which was embarrassing and totally appropriate. I looked back at the house to make sure the kids weren't watching. I didn't want the sound of my voice to be the bird's last, so I readied myself and waited for those clear, worried calls of his parents as they sat silently in the apple tree and I touched the barrel to his head.

★ ★ ★

Before we left Bobby and Gordon's apartment, my father said he doubted we would see many people on such a cold night, but he warned me and Christian not to talk to anyone if we did. When we were in New York, that was the rule. Then he zipped our coats and switched my boots, which in my haste and in the dimly lit foyer I had slipped on the wrong feet. I was also in a stupor from the night before, when Christian and I stole away to the rooftop and smoked some grass.

It had been snowing for three days and with the exception of our trip to the roof and a couple brief outings to the corner market, we had been inside for all of them. We were therefore pleased when Gordon suggested we go for a stroll down the Brooklyn Promenade. Even in his layers of clothes, Gordon appeared waif-like and his pale visage evoked that of a blue-eyed wraith. But it was without second thought that I followed him down the narrow stairwell and onto Montague Street.

When we reached the Promenade, we saw the huge flakes of snow turn and shimmer against the lights of Manhattan before dissolving into the wide, black water of the East River. Gordon leaned against the rail, pointed to an old two-story brick house, and described the horror film that had recently been made there. Houses could be terrifying places. As of that night, I had not been to the Amityville House, but when it was still possible for my parents to do things together, we drove out to the south shore of Long Island and parked in front of the house. The sun was low on the horizon, the trees were bare, and the grass was yellow. We had driven all day and now it was dusk and we stayed in the car. My mother had made sandwiches. The face of the house was dark and I looked at it once or twice and felt nervous. As I looked at the house on the Promenade, I felt a little cold was all.

My father turned me and my brother away from the house and we set out through the untracked snow. Gordon had been reading Nietzsche and my father got an earful. My brother and I ran through the storm. We were running at full speed and I fell behind my brother because he was the fastest and I adored him. I was laughing in that wild, exhausted way my son and daughter laugh and I therefore did not notice that Christian had stopped and I ran right into him. I got up and turned my hat around so that it was out of my eyes. I could smell the sweet, woolen odor of sweat rising from my open collar and I stepped out in front of my brother as if by doing so I might find the way back to the vein of ecstatic laughter.

A large man was walking toward us and his arms bulged at his sides as if he were carrying barrels under them. My father and Gordon weren't far behind, and my brother was wise enough to suggest we wait for them. When they reached us, the man was not ten yards away and my father and Gordon had time enough to guide me and my brother off to the side and thereby give the man a wide berth.

The man was massive and wearing a black wool cap and a heavy black sailor's coat. I could not see his face through the snow and dark, but I could tell he was looking at us hard as he passed. No one spoke. When we were well clear of him, I turned and stole a backward glance and saw that the man had since stopped and was watching us. My father must have already known and felt me slow because in a quiet, intense voice I had never heard he told me to turn around and keep moving.

★ ★ ★

Tosser was a terrible friend. But he did introduce me to Dee, the only Mormon girl I really wanted, but not enough to change my ways. Tosser made the mistake of bringing her to my house, to my stronghold, my place of power. Brown and I were concluding a two-week bender during which we'd start drinking right after school. By the third day we had stopped going to school and that wasn't a problem for me because no one missed me anyway, but Brown was a goody-goody, so when he started cutting class his teachers asked around and then his phone started ringing. He'd figured out when the school would call and he'd be there to answer the phone and act like he was his dad.

There was so much I didn't know back then, like where my mom was on the night Tosser showed up with Dee. I had been drinking all day and had gone upstairs and was lying on my back in the dark, trying to heal from all the self-abuse, when Dee stole away from Tosser, who sought to possess her, and came to me. My hair was longer then and she sat behind me and touched it, apparently unconcerned that at any moment Tosser might come. When I saw it was her, I was happy because it could have been someone I did not desire.

Not two weeks before the night in question, I was felt up at a Depeche Mode concert. I was standing with my friends, watching the show, when I felt something touch my inner thigh. I was in the midst of a crowd, so I dismissed it as incidental contact. But then it came again, and this time I knew it was a hand moving slowly up my thigh. Had it not stopped short of my sack, the hand would have been in for a surprise because again I wasn't wearing underwear. I figured I better find out who was attempting to play with my marbles.

Dirtbag was standing next to me and I told him I was being felt up by someone behind me. He looked back and then laughed. "You better take a look for yerself, there, Sun Jim." I turned around discreetly and saw a young blond girl about my age just loving on me hard with her eyes. I had seen that look a couple times in my life and I could live with it. What I could not live with was her six-foot-two-inch boyfriend towering behind her. I appreciated her interest on a very basic level, but she was not so great a prize that I was willing to risk being pummeled.

Not so with Dee: I would have given almost anything. I tried to. She and her family had come from Holland many years ago and had converted to Mormonism. I felt bad for them because I always assumed they didn't know any better. Her father was a good-looking guy who owned a landscaping company with an autumnal name. I worked for him for a summer and it wasn't bad work for a seventeen-year-old kid. I could get high before work if I wanted, and smoke cigarettes when Dee's father wasn't around. I didn't want him to think I was that kind of kid because I wanted to be with his daughter.

A kid named Shane ran our crew and he took a shine to me. Not the Chef-kind of shine: it was the fraternal kind where had we grown up in the same neighborhood, we would have been friends. He also knew I was with the boss's daughter and the thing was to respect a guy like that. If there were trees, we would break and lunch under them and Shane would recount his crazy stories. One of our crew was a rare, old, black guy named Ken, and he was very calm and he showed me the right way to use a rake. When he laughed, he would force the air through his nose and slap his gloves on his thigh and the dust would appear and float downwind like a golden afterthought.

Perhaps he thought as I did that Shane seemed damn good and young to have lived his storied life. As a kid, I thought of older men as potential, future mirrors, so it wasn't that I doubted Shane when I asked him for his age. "Let me put it this way," he said. "I'm old enough to know some of the finer things in life and young enough to still get away with them." I took that to mean he was about twenty-four. Whatever his age, he had done a fine job of keeping his face out of the sun.

Just before Memorial Day weekend, Dee's dad split our crew and Shane and I worked together all day installing a sprinkler system and laying sod. He leaned against the wall and sat on his boot heels and chewed tobacco while I paid my dues and dug for the water main. I didn't mind because the work made all the sense in the world. Besides, if I weren't the one digging, I'd be the one talking and I didn't think there was much I could say that would interest Shane.

We worked until dark to finish that job. Shane tested the sprinklers and when I smelled the water and saw the sun setting I got this feeling that was not quite happiness. There was still a lot of desert left then and the meadowlarks would sing out there and announce the coming night. My knees were dirt cakes and my bare chest and arms were streaked with discs and swaths of dried mud. Shane looked at me and said I looked like a warrior yard dick and I didn't disagree. He was lean and muscled with work and in his steel-toed boots, jeans with the faded chew can ring embossed in the back pocket, and untucked western-style shirt, he had an admirable roughness about him and in my mind he was a kind of promise that life was good regardless of its shape and sound and where it took hold.

"You going out tonight?" he asked as we loaded up the truck.

"I don't know. What you got going?"

Shane folded his arms across the side of the pickup and spat.

"Probably pick up a twelve-pack and drive out to the bottoms there in Riverton. There's gonna be a keg. You wanna come?"

Truth was the farther west I went, the less comfortable I felt, but I couldn't tell him that.

"Maybe. I need to see what Dee's doing."

He took his index finger, stuck it in the back of his mouth, and scooped out his wad of chewing tobacco.

"Okay, well, shoot yourself. If you change your mind, you know how to get out there, right?"

I nodded that I did and then he took out his can, held it between his thumb and middle finger, and shook his wrist back and forth, snapping the can against his index finger, and packed the chaw. Shane had it down.

"Dip?" he asked, offering me the can.

"No, thanks. I can't chew Cope. That shit turns me green."

Shane smirked and took a pinch and sat it between his front lip and gum. "Shit would turn you green," he said, taking issue with my comparison.

He dropped me off at the top of 9800 South and I grabbed my lunch box and water cooler from the back of his old white Ford. He had been watching me in the rearview mirror and when he saw that I was clear he waved and drove off. It was full dark by then and as his brake lights receded into the pitch, I thought of that pig gazing from the upstairs window in Amityville, and I wondered what it would be like to see the world through eyes of fire.

Four days later I drove into the foothills above Deer Hollow to meet the crew at the job site. A heavy May rain had soaked the valley the day before and the water had washed dirt into the street. The sun had just crested the horizon south of Lone Peak and everything that still held rain reflected the light and it was not the malicious kind of shining. Lots had been cut out of the foothills and it was a wonder that the mountain did not slide. I saw the boss's truck parked in front of a house. It was loaded with twenty-foot sections of sprinkler pipe and trailing a ditch-witch on a flatbed. Besides the boss, Shane was the only man trained on the ditch-witch, but his truck was not there.

I parked down the street and grabbed my gloves, lunch, and water jug and walked toward the boss's truck. He was standing in front of it talking with a man who I guessed was the customer. They had spread plans across the hood and were pointing at them. When the boss saw me he gestured to the back and then returned to his discussion. He was one of those guys who was poker-faced all the time and I could never tell how he felt about me. I didn't blame him. I wasn't sure myself.

The other men had placed their lunch pails and water jugs on the front porch out of the sun and I put mine with them and walked around back. Ken and the others were standing in a broken circle, alternately smoking and talking and staring at the ground. The young men were slouching and they looked wrecked by the long weekend. I stuffed my gloves in my back pocket and took my place in the circle. Ken took off his glasses and used his massive thumb to clear his eyes.

"You see the boss?" he asked, returning the glasses to his face.

"Yeah," I said.

Ken cleared his throat.

"I guess he didn't tell you about Shane?"

I looked at the other men and they looked at me flatly.

"What about Shane?"

Ken scratched his throat and I could hear the stiff, dry sound of stubble.

"Fool done got himself killed."

A few days later I would learn that Shane had been speeding south on I-15 after a fight with his girlfriend and a state trooper had clocked him going a hundred miles an hour. When the trooper tried to pull him over, Shane made a run for it. He took the Draper off-ramp going about sixty miles an hour, rolled, and was ejected. Troopers found his body fifty feet from the vehicle, lying in the grass. So ruined was he by the metal and the glass that it took them a couple minutes to understand what they were seeing.

I dreamed about Shane only once. I flew above him as he drove his big old eight-banger down a two-track that had tall grass growing down the center of it. I could hear the grass hiss as the truck passed over it. We went on like that until the road opened onto a dark field. The horizon beyond was deep blue and I could see the profiles of large, sleeping animals. Shane drove out into the center of them, put the truck in park, and turned off the ignition. One by one, the beasts lifted their heads and sniffed the air. I guessed they liked what they smelled because they converged on the truck and within moments it was gone.

★ ★ ★

However much I wanted otherwise, I knew Dee and I didn't have a chance. I was unwholesome and had hang-ups. And I wasn't Mormon. I navigated the world with a foggy brain and bleary eyes. I remember her lying on the sandy shoal at the inlet of the reservoir. She had long, brown hair, arms, and legs. When I see us there over twenty-five summers ago, I feel the awful void of something left unsaid and unfinished. Remembered beauty may not dissolve bone nor swell the nerves, but it still shapes the present.

Absent and unchangeable, the past itself is a mass extinction of increments and the memories are trace fossils eroded by the air and sun and water, and by the worst kind of desire, which is desire that will never be realized. Now the months and the years lie on the surface. They are so fresh and warm; I can almost live them twice. But recollecting a night a quarter-century ago, the night of the Big Dance? Past pain and pleasure is akin to the present: it makes for a soft loam. Easy digging. In two hours, I've dug down over nine thousand days.

On the seam between winter and spring, the ground is still frozen and blackened with snowmelt. As I finished my fourth beer on Brody's back porch, I closed my eyes and enjoyed the sweet coolness of the air as it came down out of the foothills behind his house. The sun had just dropped below the western horizon and its remnant light bathed the green hills and dark switchbacks made by deer that had come down from the once snow-covered mountains in search of food. I was still enrolled in public high school then, although I rarely made it through a day without coming late or leaving early or wishing I had.

As of the night of the Big Dance, things had already gone south with Dee and I intended to go and use the words I had found to lay bare the smitten heaviness of my drunken heart. Brody had quit school by then and was working full time with the Hippie as an auto mechanic downtown. He had nothing to lose so far as public education was concerned. The system had done all that it was going to do for him. After we were sufficiently sauced, he agreed to drive me and my other friend Sport to the dance. We stuffed a couple beers in our pockets and climbed into the Porsche Eater. Sport was a couple years younger than me and Brody and so, though beautiful, he was something of a child.

This did not keep him from pursuing Faux with pubescent vigor. His timing could not have been worse, however, for not only had Faux just lived through the corporeal ravages of Dirtbag and the Priottzo, she had also spent considerable energy delicately rejecting Brown's advances. Soon after these trials, Faux had reassessed and reasserted her commitment to all things Mormon. All her life she had been a tough crack to nut, and by God she would be so again. Thus there would be no more spreading of legs and she would surround herself with her own kind: the beautiful and visibly uncomplicated Mormon boys and girls. Of course Sport was not privy to any of this knowledge, and even if he were, it would not have stopped him because it has never stopped anyone. He was a bee at work in the cherry blossoms. The only reason I knew of this new status was because I had been suffering from it myself since Dee and I called it quits.

Human strategy has always been to destroy or abandon what cannot be controlled. Great for dealing with cigarettes, drugs, and alcohol; not so great for dealing with Dee and human relationships. In a doomed attempt to bring her around, I suggested we take a break and she thought about it for a few seconds and then agreed. And that was it. Totally unlike life, which, if we're lucky, is really just one long goodbye. A proper goodbye to a beauty like Dee should have taken years.

I didn't do many things that I would later regret. I just said them. I was a sayer, a talker, and in a matter of seconds I talked myself right out of a relationship with the most beautiful girl I had ever seen. That was not so unusual. Nor was my belief in second chances, and if words got me into this mess, then by Brigham Young's beard, they would get me out of it. Instead of devising and rehearsing what I would say, I knocked down beers and stupefied my tongue. Maybe I would have found the right combination of words to woo her back, but I would never get the opportunity.

When we pulled into the school parking lot, the dance was almost over and small groups of kids were standing around or filing out of the building and they all seemed so unburdened. Initially Brody idled through the lot, the big car rumbling like the beast that it was. But then he saw some pretty girls and got a hair up his ass and he punched the throttle so that the car fish-tailed. No sooner had we come out of it than we were descended upon by a contingent of three vice principals. They wore black trousers, sweater vests, and jackets, and they packed Walkie-talkies. Were it not for their pale faces, they would have been completely encrypted in the night. They were like the commandos of the public education system. Sometimes during school we would see them on the roof, from which vantage point they would scan the parking lot with binoculars, looking for kids skipping class or smoking drugs.

Little did they know that we had found a place *inside* the school, the edifice of their authority, a place where we could smoke pot right under the teacher's nose, or rather, right above it since in this particular room we would stand on the counter, remove the ceiling panel, and blow our hits up into the roof, where they would rise into the rafters and intoxicate the insect life. Whatever we had gotten away with had now caught up with us because we were surrounded and I knew my time at that school was done.

I stuffed my beers under Brody's seat and looked out the window. I was mildly relieved to see Vice Principal Sarks, in whose office I had spent many days with my mother, who did everything she could to keep me in school. It wasn't that I thought Sarks was going to be sympathetic. It was that I knew he was nonviolent, unlike Vice Principal Philpot, a former Marine sergeant who, so far as anyone with eyes could tell, had no business working with kids.

I had witnessed his handiwork one morning when Tosser and I got to school late and were headed to art class. I saw Philpot lingering outside his office door, so I knew to keep moving, but Tosser had stopped to chat up some sweet thing and Philpot went to work. The girl must have seen him first because she moved off and disappeared into the locker rows just as he rounded the corner. Tosser saw him and started walking, but it was too late. Philpot had him in his sights and nothing Tosser could say or do was going to change what was about to happen. "Hey, young man," Philpot barked. "Get your skinny butt to class." Tosser looked back, but he didn't respond and that was the only reason Philpot needed to make good on his rage, which had no more to do with Tosser than it did with the sun in the sky. It didn't help that Tosser literally had a skinny butt, thin legs, and a swagger that accentuated his chest. The guy couldn't take two steps without appearing to challenge the world.

"Hold up, you little pecker head," Philpot yelled as he damn near broke into a run.

"I'm going to class," Tosser said, in strange mixture of hurt and anger.

By then Philpot had caught up with him, taken him by the arm, and walked him hard to the wall. I could see Tosser's whole demeanor change from flight to fight. I'll never forget the sight of that little guy standing there red-faced and fists clenched, his jaw jutting in defiance of the huge blockhead that towered above him. Tosser kept trying to leave the wall, but Philpot would push him back until, finally, Philpot got a hold of himself and told Tosser to get his ass to the office. I was glad when he did because I was sure they were going to come to blows. Tosser had a lot of hurt and rage to give. The only reason I think he didn't go ballistic was because he knew Philpot would repay his fury a hundredfold.

When Sarks and I finally made eye contact, his face dropped into a look of resignation. I had disappointed him and broken the rules for the last time. There would be no negotiations. We got out and they quickly found the beers and placed them on the roof of the car. Brody had only drunk a beer or so, and they found nothing near or on him. And given that he wasn't a student at the school, they avoided the headache he undoubtedly represented and turned him loose. But Sport and I were students, well-known students, in fact.

A police cruiser was already there when we arrived. I knew Sarks intended to put me in it, but I had to piss first and so he agreed to walk me inside. He didn't hold my arm or anything because I had nowhere to run. The other kids looked at me with pitiful expressions. Sarks knew how things worked, that public humiliation was a powerful punishment. But I didn't hold that against him. He did what he could for me. He might have even saved my life.

One morning when I was again late to class and getting my books from my locker, back before things took a turn for the worse, this Rocker kid appeared at the end of the row. I had not said two words to this kid in my entire life, but he had it in for me, I guessed, because I did things like wear short hair, listen to the Sex Pistols, ride a skateboard, and peg my Levis. The locker row was poorly lit, so it was difficult to see his eyes. But then he smiled and I saw that he had a knife.

I grabbed my skateboard out of the locker and held it tightly by the back truck. I made sure he could see it. We stood there for a few seconds looking at each other while the morning announcements were made over the intercom by the student body president, who I envied for the first time in my life. Shortly after that a couple of girls appeared behind the Rocker and entered the row, giggling and carrying on about only they knew what. He nodded at me as if to say *We'll finish this later*, and I thought *The fuck we will* and went right to Sarks's office and told him what had just happened. Sarks asked me for the kid's name, which I didn't know, but I did know he was likely the leader of the Rockers and how he came to focus on me was a puzzle to us both because I had never been so important as that.

Things cooled off for a while, so I figured Sarks must have talked to him. Over the next few weeks I started to hear rumblings and rumors of a big fight that was going to take place between the Rockers and the Skaters/Punkers, but I ignored them because personally I hadn't been given reason to do otherwise. I realized the depth of my mistake on the last day of school as Brody, Tosser, and I were crossing the grass toward Brody's car, which was parked across the street. "What the hell is going on over there?" Brody asked. Thirty or forty kids—Rockers, Preppies, Punkers, Shit Kickers, Jocks, the works—had amassed in the main parking lot and from the looks of things the gathering was not a happy one.

We were about halfway to the car when the knife-wielding Rocker saw us and yelled a war cry and about a third of the throng broke away and started running toward us, screaming and yelling profanities. I still couldn't believe these assholes were actually going to attack us in broad daylight on school property, so initially I concurred with Tosser when he said, "I'm not tucking tail and running from those fucking Rock dogs." By then Brody was almost at the car, which was good, because when the Rockers were within twenty yards, Tosser and I could see their faces and we saw they were serious.

We had just climbed into Brody's car and locked the doors when about six of them jumped on top of the car and crawled around like amputee spiders. Brody revved the engine and they scuttled out of the way when he dropped the car in gear. We blew out of there like aliens fleeing a hostile planet, blasting them with a heavy spray of rocks and dirt. It was important to leave them with something they understood.

Sport was already in the back of the police cruiser when I returned from the bathroom, but we didn't talk. The cop told us our parents were on their way. I glanced at Sport and he looked straight ahead. He came from one of those rare households that had two parents, and he was in for it. I also knew what was going to happen to me: I would suffer my mother's angry words and scowling face. I would be grounded for a month, which would turn into two weeks, which would become a few days. I don't know how she raised three teenagers by herself. Love? Luck? Absentia? All of it. Either way, I was unconcerned. But then Dee and Faux walked out of the building arm-in-arm with two of the most beautiful Mormon boys to have ever walked the halls of that school.

They were transcendent not only because of their beauty—their shiny hair and perfect teeth; one had even dared proclaim his dream of becoming a news anchor so people could look at him—but because they had graduated the year before. These guys were untouchable and free. And there I was, sitting in a cage inside a prison in a world I saw too little of to understand.

As the four of them came down the walkway, laughing and joshing in that unequivocally Mormon sort of way, I watched Dee's eyes and hoped to hell she wouldn't see me. But of course it wouldn't be my life if she didn't. And so just as they turned up the walkway, Dee glanced into the back of the car and looked me square in the eye for a second or two. And that was enough. I knew what she meant. Nothing had changed. *Okay, Okay. You got me. I'm lost. I admit it.*

★ ★ ★

Robins are butchers with wings.

★ ★ ★

It is winter. The Wasatch Mountains rise in the background. They look cold and bands of fresh clouds drift across them. I am driving through the slushy streets to a sledding hill not far from our house in Mill Creek. Kim is sitting next to me, holding my hand in her lap. When we arrive, a light snow is floating through the gray air. We put on the kids' boots, coats, and mittens and take the sled from the car. Several children with red cheeks and hair wet from the falling snow stand with their parents or older brothers and sisters and ready themselves for the icy plummet, while others, having already descended, drag their sleds up the hill.

Concerned that the speed from the top will be too great, Kim and I convince Wilder to begin beneath a maple tree midway down the slope. Somehow it still has leaves on it. Wilder agrees and soon he is racing down, clutching the sides of the sled. I know the phraseology of his body and I can tell he is terrified. When the sled finally stops, I am sure he'll be finished. That is the mistake I keep making.

I call down to him and ask if he enjoyed the ride. He pushes back his hat and now I can see his clear, blue eyes. "I want to do it again!" he shouts, gleefully. I glance at Kim and she is holding Greer and they are squinting in the snow and smiling. Together they give beauty a depth and fullness all their own.

Then Kim says something in Greer's ear and she throws back her head and laughs and laughs in that loving way that, if we were lucky, we might have known as children. And suddenly the sound is muted, everything slows down, and I hear this voice say, *This is your chance to love other people.*

When I look back at Wilder, he is lumbering up the hill, taking his own sweet time. I walk down to help him with his sled. "I can do it," he says. The other children race past us, their screams of laughter hanging in the sharp, December air. And I think I've seen it all. But then I look at Wilder and his face is red and bright and he wears this wide, knowing smile.

I don't know why, but the look unsettles me. A heaviness grows in my chest and I can't decide if I am going to cry or laugh or stop breathing. We get to the top of the hill and I hold the sled for him while he climbs on.

"Let go," he says, laughing. "Let go."

"Are you sure you'll be okay?" I ask.

"Yes, but watch me, Dad, watch me!" he yells, looking back. "Watch as I take my turn."